FOOTPRINT READING LIBRARY
COLLECTION
LEVEL 1

Rob Waring, *Series Editor*

HEINLE
CENGAGE Learning™

Australia • Brazil • Japan • Korea • Mexico • Singapore • Spain • United Kingdom • United States

HEINLE
CENGAGE Learning™

Footprint Reading Library Collection: Level 1
Series Editor: Rob Waring

Publisher: *Sherrise Roehr*
Associate Development Editor: *Catherine McCue*
Editorial Assistant: *Heidi North*
Assistant Editor: *Marissa Petrarca*
Director of Marketing: *Jim McDonough*
Product Marketing Manager: *Katie Kelley*
Content Project Manager: *Jin Hock Tan*
Print Buyer: *Susan Carroll*

Library of Congress Control Number: 2006908272
ISBN 13: 978-1-4240-4513-6
ISBN 10: 1-4240-4513-4

Heinle
20 Channel Center Street
Boston, Massachusetts 02210
USA

Cengage Learning is a leading provider of customized learning solutions with office locations around the globe, including Singapore, the United Kingdom, Australia, Mexico, Brazil, and Japan. Locate our local office at: **international.cengage.com/region**

Cengage Learning products are represented in Canada by Nelson Education, Ltd.

Visit Heinle online at **elt.heinle.com**
Visit our corporate website at **www.cengage.com**

Printed in the United States of America..

1 2 3 4 5 6 7 8 9 10 — 13 12 11 10 09

Contents

Incredible Animals

Fascinating Places

Remarkable People

Contents (continued)

Exciting Activities

Amazing Science

Arctic
Whale Danger!

Rob Waring, *Series Editor*

HEINLE
CENGAGE Learning

Australia • Brazil • Japan • Korea • Mexico • Singapore • Spain • United Kingdom • United States

Words to Know

This story is set in the
Arctic **Ocean**.

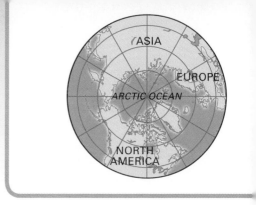

A **The Arctic Shore.** Write each word in the picture next to the
correct definition.

1. the land next to the ocean: _____.
2. a large white sea animal: _____.
3. hard pieces of water formed in the cold: _____.
4. big stones that you find sometimes find near the sea: _____.
5. a part of the sea that is nearly closed in by land: _____.
6. a large sea animal that has a long object on its head: _____.

The Arctic Shore

B **Arctic Animals.** Look at the pictures and captions. Complete the paragraph with the correct form of the **bolded** words.

Narwhals have a long tusk.

Codfish swimming in the ocean.

An **adult beluga whale** and her **calf**.

Many kinds of whales live in the Arctic Ocean. 1)_____ are very big and white. 2)_____ have a long tusk. A baby whale is called a 3)_____. Most whales like to eat fish. One kind of fish they eat is called 4)_____.

Beluga whales are very social animals. This means that they like to be around other whales. Their relationships with the whales around them are very strong. A mother and her calf will often swim together for three years. Beluga whale calves are gray when they are born. They turn white, like the ice around them, when they become adults.

It may seem like the beluga whales have a very happy life, but sometimes this isn't the case …

 CD 1, Track 1

A5

On one particular day, a group of beluga whales is swimming in the bay. When the **tide**[1] goes out, the adult belugas are able to swim back to deeper water.

However, one young beluga has gone too far onto the shore. It can't get back to the water. Suddenly, play time becomes a **race against time!**[2]

---

[1]**tide:** the regular rising and falling of the ocean
[2]**race against time:** need to hurry or act quickly

The Sun now becomes the whale's biggest danger. It's very hot on the young beluga's body. The whale could easily **sunburn**[3], get too hot, and die. The young beluga has nothing to cover it. It's totally helpless. The other belugas can only watch and wait as the calf tries to move.

As the beluga calf moves around on the shore, the rocks cut its skin. More and more time passes. The minutes slowly turn into hours. There's nothing that the whale can do for now. It can only wait for the tide to come back.

Everyone has **made a mistake**[4] in their life. However, this mistake could be deadly for the little beluga. Finally, the tide starts coming back. But will it be soon enough to help the baby beluga?

---

[3]**sunburn:** when the skin becomes red and hot from the sun
[4]**make a mistake:** do something wrong

Predict

Answer the questions. Then, scan page A11 to check your answers.

1. What will happen to the beluga calf?

2. Why do you think that?

A10

Slowly the sea starts to come back onto the shore. The water brings the very tired beluga back to life. It begins to move. Then, it begins to push … and push … and push. With one last energetic push, the beluga is **free**[5]! At last, it's able to return to the sea.

The young beluga quickly joins the other whales in the deep water once again. The young calf is fine. Perhaps it has learned something from this bad experience. Perhaps it will be more careful the next time it's near the shore!

---

[5]**free:** able to go where it wants

Young belugas are not the only arctic whales that can get in trouble. The narwhal is another type of whale that lives in the Arctic Ocean. They are a very unusual kind of whale. They have a tusk, or horn, that can grow as long as **nine feet!**[6] The tusk is actually a kind of tooth that grows through the narwhal's top **lip.**[7] Before, no one knew why the narwhals had this tusk. Most people thought that the whales only used it to fight other whales. However, scientists now think that the tusk helps narwhals sense environmental conditions, like **temperature.**[8]

---

[6]**nine feet:** 2.74 meters
[7]**lip:** the area around the mouth
[8]**temperature:** how hot or cold something is

A14

Narwhals usually swim in small groups. However, on this day the number of narwhals swimming together is much larger. The exact number may vary, but sometimes the group might grow to more than a hundred whales! The whales are swimming together as they look for a favorite food—codfish.

After a while, the narwhals follow a group of codfish into the bay. But they're taking a big risk. The bay has ice all around it. If the ice moves and closes the opening to the bay, the whales could become **trapped**.[9]

---

[9]**trapped:** unable to move

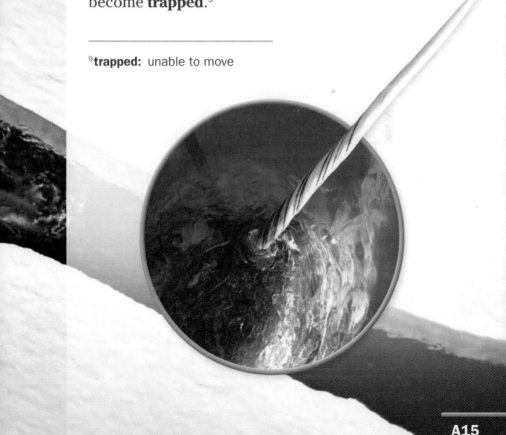

And that's exactly what happens! Suddenly, the ice moves in and closes off the way out to the open sea. The narwhals can't get out of the bay. They're trapped! Not even their long tusks can help them now ...

All the narwhals now have to swim in a very small area of water that has no ice on it. It's a very difficult situation for the narwhals. Whales **breathe oxygen.**[10] If the ice moves closer and covers the water, the narwhals can't come out of the water. They won't be able to get air! They'll have to swim out from under the ice to find it or they'll die. Will the whales be able to find air in time?

---

[10]**breathe oxygen:** use air in their bodies

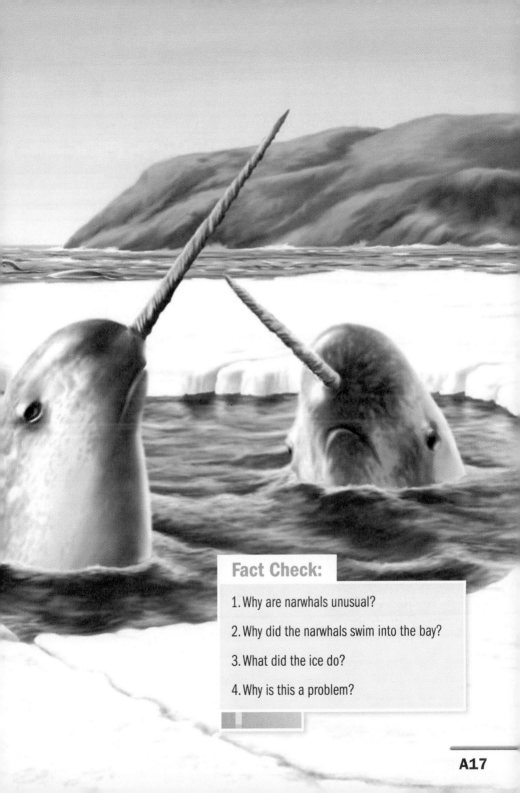

Fact Check:

1. Why are narwhals unusual?

2. Why did the narwhals swim into the bay?

3. What did the ice do?

4. Why is this a problem?

Suddenly, the ice moves. The way out of the bay and into the ocean is open again. Finally, the narwhals are not trapped anymore. They are free. They're free to look for fish. Free to swim the seas. Free to do whatever they want to do—with that very unusual tusk!

A19

After You Read

1. The beluga whale is _____ very social animal.
   A. the
   B. an
   C. that
   D. a

2. What color is an adult beluga whale?
   A. gray-white
   B. gray
   C. white
   D. none of the above

3. On page A7, 'it' refers to:
   A. the shore
   B. a baby beluga
   C. the tide
   D. deeper water

4. What is a good heading for page A8?
   A. Young Whale in Trouble
   B. The Tide Comes Back
   C. Adult Beluga Makes Deadly Mistake
   D. Whale Finds New Home

5. After the tide comes back, where does the young whale go?
   A. to the rocks
   B. to the other whales
   C. to the shore
   D. to the ice

6. What is one known way the narwhals use their tusks?
   A. to fight other whales
   B. to swim better
   C. to get codfish
   D. no one knows

7. What's a good heading for page A12?
   A. Looking for Codfish
   B. Ice Moves in Suddenly
   C. The Arctic Ocean
   D. An Unusual, Whale

8. On page A15, 'taking a big risk' can be replaced by:
   A. being difficult
   B. very unusual
   C. possibly in danger
   D. looking for fish

9. The narwhals become trapped in the _____.
   A. shore
   B. ocean
   C. open sea
   D. bay

10. How do the narwhals get free?
   A. The tide comes in.
   B. The ice opens a way.
   C. They swim under the ice.
   D. The ice moves closer.

11. Which is NOT true for both narwhals and belugas in this story?
   A. They breathe oxygen.
   B. They like to swim with others.
   C. They live in the Arctic Ocean.
   D. They have tusks.

Visiting
the Arctic

Y ou've seen pictures of beluga whales and narwhals. You've read something about how they live in the Arctic Ocean. But have you ever thought about visiting the Arctic yourself? Every year thousands of people do. They get there on ships that leave from cities in Canada, Russia, and parts of Europe. Here are some questions that people planning a trip to the Arctic often ask.

Tourists on a ship in the Arctic Ocean

Q: WHAT KINDS OF SHIPS GO TO THE ARCTIC?

A: Only special ships can go to the Arctic. They must be very strong because of all the ice in the Arctic Ocean. Many of the ships are also quite small. The largest ones hold no more than 100 people. Most of them hold around 50 people. Some ships leave from small towns in northern Canada. Tourists usually have to fly there from Montreal. People can also leave from cities in northern Europe or the northern part of Russia.

Q: WHEN IS THE BEST TIME TO GO?

A: The best time to visit the Arctic Ocean is during the months of July, and August. During these months, the temperatures are usually above 45 degrees Fahrenheit during the day. In January and February, the temperature can be very cold. During these months, ice covers many parts of the Arctic Ocean and ships cannot pass through. In some places this ice can be several feet thick.

"Most travelers say that their trip to the Arctic was very interesting."

Q: WHAT DO PEOPLE DO ON THE SHIP?

A: Most ships offer classes every day. People can learn about the things they will see on shore. They can also learn about the history of the area. Who first found the area? What did they see there? There are also often classes about local sea animals, like birds, whales, or codfish. All of these animals are common in the Arctic. Most travelers say that their trip to the Arctic was very interesting. Some think it's the best vacation they've ever taken.

CD 1, Track 2

Word Count: 312
Time: _____

Vocabulary List

adult (A: 3, 4, 7)
bay (A: 2, 15, 16, 17, 18)
beluga whale (A: 2, 3, 4, 7, 8, 11, 12)
breathe oxygen (A: 16)
calf (A: 3, 4, 8, 11)
codfish (A: 3, 15)
free (A: 11, 18)
ice (A: 2, 15, 16, 18)
lip (A: 12)
make (a) mistake (A: 8)
narwhal (A: 2, 3, 12, 15, 16, 18)
ocean (A: 2, 3, 18)
race against time (A: 7)
rocks (A: 2, 8)
shore (A: 2, 11)
sunburn (A: 8)
swim (A: 3, 7, 15, 16)
temperature (A: 12)
tide (A: 7, 8)
trapped (A: 15, 16, 18)

Happy Elephants

Rob Waring, *Series Editor*

HEINLE
CENGAGE Learning™

Australia • Brazil • Japan • Korea • Mexico • Singapore • Spain • United Kingdom • United States

B1

Words to Know

This story is set in the United States (U.S.). It happens in the state of Maryland, in a city called Baltimore.

A **Elephants in the Wild.** Read the facts about elephants. Then, write each underlined word or phrase next to the correct definition.

When elephants are <u>in the wild</u>, they are free.
Elephants live in families, like <u>humans</u> do.
Several elephant families often come together to make a <u>herd</u>.
When it is hot, elephants like to get into water and <u>mud</u>.
Elephants use their <u>trunk</u> to pick up things.

1. a soft combination of water and earth: _____

2. people: _____

3. the long powerful nose of an elephant: _____

4. in natural conditions: _____

5. a large group of animals of the same type that live and eat together: _____

A Herd of Elephants

B Elephants at Work. Look at the pictures and read the paragraph. Then, complete the paragraph with the words in the box.

gentle	captivity	trainer	circus	zoo

If elephants aren't in the wild, they are usually in (1) _____ and are kept by people. These elephants often live in a zoo or work in a circus. A (2) _____ is a place where many animals live and people can go to see them. Many people love elephants because they're usually very friendly and (3) _____. Other elephants work in a (4) _____. This is a kind of show in which people and animals perform. An animal (5) _____ works with these elephants. This person teaches the elephants what to do in the show.

An Elephant in the Zoo

An Animal Trainer with a Circus Elephant

Elephants are very large animals, but they are also very gentle. They are important to humans too. Elephants and people have worked together for over 2,000 years. However, when they work with people, the elephants are usually not in the wild. They are usually in captivity and working in zoos or circuses.

Over these 2,000 years, people have learned a lot about the way elephants act. However, there is one question that people are still concerned about: How can people keep elephants happy when they are in captivity?

 CD 1, Track 03

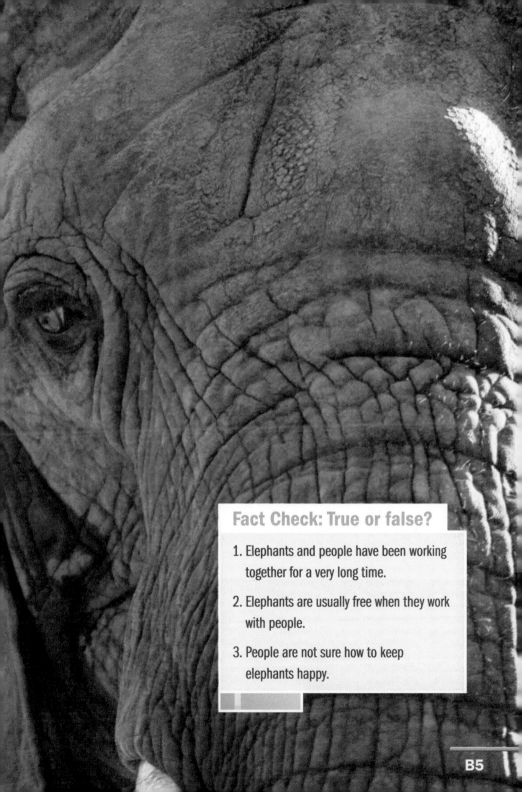

Fact Check: True or false?

1. Elephants and people have been working together for a very long time.

2. Elephants are usually free when they work with people.

3. People are not sure how to keep elephants happy.

Mike **Hackenberger**[1] is a skilled animal trainer at the Baltimore Zoo. He works hard to make sure his elephants are healthy and seem happy. His elephants even seem to say 'hello' when Hackenberger says, "OK, everyone, trunk foot salute!"

"We make sure teeth are where they're supposed to be, [they] don't have **ingrown feet**[2] … " he explains. "This is all that good **husbandry**[3] stuff," he adds. Hackenberger is responsible for teaching other zoo workers how to recognize a happy elephant. Part of his method for doing this is to talk to the elephants. "Oh you're happy … " he says to one elephant. "Hear that?" he asks as the elephant makes a low noise, "That's a happy sound," he reports. "That's a good sound."

---

[1]**Hackenberger:** [hækənbɜrgər]
[2]**ingrown feet:** an uncomfortable condition of the foot
[3]**husbandry:** animal care

A Trunk-Foot Salute

But can elephants really be happy? Do animals have feelings? If so, are their feelings the same as people's feelings? There's a big discussion about this subject. Many people who work closely with animals say that they do have feelings and can experience happiness. These people think animals are just like humans. Other people are not so certain.

Predict

On the next page you will read about one way that Mike Hackenberger makes elephants feel good. What do you think it is? Scan page B10 to check your answer.

There is one thing that everyone agrees on when they talk about elephants. Elephants seem happier—and safer—if their home in the zoo or circus is very similar to their life among their herd in the wild. Today, zoos work hard to make elephants feel as 'at home' as possible.

Hackenberger also talks to the elephants, and this may help comfort them. "Head over, let's go kids," he says to a group of elephants. "Let's go, **Fatman**![4] Let's go … watch yourself," he says with a smile. He also encourages the animals as they move along, "We're walking, guys. Come on, **Funnyface**,[5] good boy," he says.

_____

[4]**Fatman:** a pet name that Hackenberger uses for a particular elephant
[5]**Funnyface:** a pet name that Hackenberger uses for a particular elephant

According to Hackenberger, the training of elephants has improved in recent years. He explains, "I'll tell you … ten, fifteen, twenty-five years ago, some of the **techniques**[6] were a bit **barbaric**.[7] We've **walked away from**[8] that … society's walked away from [treating animals like that]." That's news that makes everybody happy.

---

[6]**technique:** a way of doing something that needs skill
[7]**barbaric:** very unkind
[8]**walk away from:** leave behind; forget

One important fact about elephants is that they are social animals. This means that they usually live in families and herds. They need other elephants. Therefore, if they are alone for a long time, they seem to be unhappy and they can start to act in an unusual way.

Hackenberger talks about one elephant, called **Limba**.[9] Limba was alone for 30 years in a zoo in northern **Quebec**,[10] and she didn't do very well by herself. Hackenberger then tells the story of how two other elephants came to live with Limba. They were only two days old at the time. He thinks Limba 'fell in love' with the two young elephants. He also feels that is the reason Limba became happier, and more like a normal elephant.

---

[9] **Limba:** [lɪmbə]
[10] **Quebec:** a part of Canada

Limba fell in love with the two young elephants.

When he is training elephants, Hackenberger talks to them a lot. He's very gentle with them as well. Most importantly, he lets them do things that they do when they are free, in the wild.

For example, elephants love to swim and play in the mud. "Do you? You want to go swimming?" Hackenberger asks the elephants. "**Absolutely**,"[11] he answers for one of them as the elephant actually **nods his head**![12] "Let's get in the water," he says and takes them to the mud hole. The animals really seem to like this pleasant activity.

---

[11]**absolutely:** yes(!); of course!
[12]**nod (ones) head:** move one's head up and down to say yes

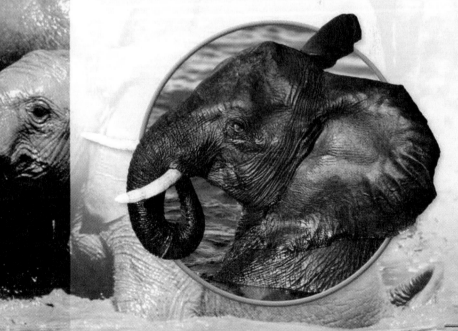

So what is the answer to the question: How can people keep elephants happy when they are in captivity? For Hackenberger, the answer is not difficult. He believes that elephants need to learn how to be elephants, just as they are in the wild.

"Are they trained?" he asks a person visiting the zoo. "I think so," she replies. "They're trained to be elephants!" he explains. He then tells one of his very large friends, "Just be an elephant!" With Hackenberger's help, it certainly seems as though his animals are very, very happy elephants!

Summarize

What does Hackenberger think about how to keep elephants happy? Summarize this in one sentence.

After You Read

1. On page B4, the word 'gentle' means:
   A. lively
   B. angry
   C. wild
   D. kind

2. There is one question about elephants that people _____ agree on: can elephants be happy?
   A. will
   B. cannot
   C. do
   D. can

3. Which is NOT one way Hackenberger tries to makes his elephants healthy and happy?
   A. He talks to them.
   B. He checks their teeth and feet.
   C. He takes them to the circus.
   D. He trains them well.

4. A good heading for page B6 is:
   A. Man Trains Elephants to Make Happy Sounds
   B. Trainer and Elephants Happy at Seattle Zoo
   C. Trainer Talks to Elephants Too Much
   D. Elephants Are Happy with Caring Trainer

5. Most people who work with animals think that animals:
   A. have feelings
   B. are always happy
   C. are happier than children
   D. cannot have feelings

6. On page B8, who is 'they'?
   A. trainers
   B. feelings
   C. animals
   D. people

7. Society has walked away from _____ animal training techniques.
   A. easy
   B. unkind
   C. good
   D. any

8. What is the meaning of 'unusual' on page B14?
   A. good
   B. bad
   C. boring
   D. happy

9. Why did Limba fall in love with the young elephants?
   A. Because elephants love all young things.
   B. Because elephants are social animals.
   C. Because young elephants are good trainers.
   D. Because she enjoys living alone.

10. Which of the following is something elephants do in the wild?
    A. swim and play in the mud
    B. communicate with people
    C. play together with trainers
    D. fall in love with people

11. What does Hackenberger believe about making elephants happy in captivity?
    A. Elephants can't be happy in a zoo.
    B. Elephants are happy anywhere they can be elephants.
    C. Elephants are happy in captivity if they have a trainer.
    D. Elephants are happiest when they are alone.

Be an Elephant Keeper

Every year thousands of young people leave school for a few weeks or months and enjoy an unusual type of educational program. What they learn during this time does not come from books. They learn new things by living in a different country and doing unusual jobs. There are several organizations that help students find the experience they are looking for. The job description chart below shows a few possibilities for students.

Country	Job	Time	Description
India	Teaching young children	Two months	• Teach music and art • Help children to learn how to communicate
Ghana	Health care worker	Three months	• See how doctors work in a less developed country • Help care for some people
Thailand	Saving elephants	Three weeks	• Cleaning elephants • Helping train elephants

A job can be a learning experience.

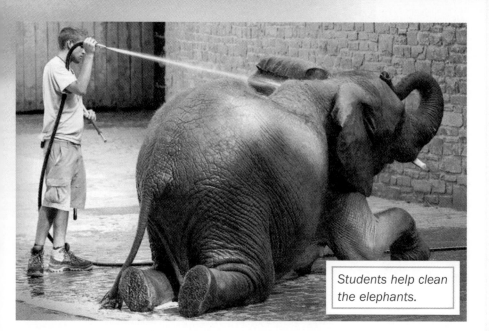

Students help clean the elephants.

One interesting possibility is helping elephants in Thailand. Most people think of elephants as animals in zoos or circuses. However, many elephants in Thailand are no longer kept in captivity. Now, hundreds of them are homeless. These gentle animals are often found on the streets as they do not have owners to care for them. Although they may look well, they are often in poor health and don't have enough to eat.

One center in Thailand cares for these elephants. It provides a safe and natural living space for them. When they are at the center, they stay in a building but they are still free to walk around. Students come from all over the world to help here. The student helpers work with the elephant keepers. These keepers train the students in caring for the elephants. In the morning, they go to the forest together and lead the elephants to the center. They clean them and give them food. In the afternoon, they take the animals back into the forest for the night. Helping at the center is interesting and the young people learn a lot.

CD 1, Track 04

Word Count: 322
Time: _____

Vocabulary List

absolutely (B: 17)

barbaric (B: 13)

captivity (B: 3, 4, 18)

circus (B: 3, 4, 10)

gentle (B: 3, 17)

herd (B: 2, 10, 14)

humans (B: 2, 4, 8)

husbandry (B: 6)

in the wild (B: 2, 3, 4, 10, 12, 17, 18)

ingrown feet (B: 6)

mud (B: 2, 17)

technique (B: 13)

train (B: 3, 6, 13, 17, 18)

trunk (B: 2, 6)

walk away from (B: 13)

zoo (B: 3, 4, 6, 10, 14)

Monkey
PARTY

Rob Waring, *Series Editor*

HEINLE
CENGAGE Learning™

Australia • Brazil • Japan • Korea • Mexico • Singapore • Spain • United Kingdom • United States

Words to Know

This story is set in Thailand. It happens in Lopburi [lʌpbʊri], a town north of Bangkok. People and things from Thailand are called 'Thai.'

A **Things in Lopburi.** Read the sentences. Label the pictures with the <u>underlined</u> words.

A <u>banquet</u> is a very big dinner, with lots of food.
A <u>cake</u> is something sweet to eat.
A <u>festival</u> is a big, public party.
A <u>monkey</u> is a small animal.
A <u>shrine</u> is a place that is related to a god.

1. _____

2. _____

3. _____

4. _____

5. _____

B **Buddhism.** Read the paragraph. Then complete the definitions with the words in the box.

   Buddhists believe in the teachings of a special man named 'Buddha.' Buddhists have many traditions. One Buddhist tradition is to give food to monkeys. This is because of a famous legend. In this legend, a monkey was a hero. Because of this, Buddhists think helping monkeys will bring them good karma. They think good karma will bring them happiness.

Buddhist	hero	karma	legend	tradition

1. Good _____ is a good feeling or kind of luck.
2. A _____ is the main good person in a story.
3. A _____ is a way of doing things year after year.
4. A _____ is a story from a long time ago.
5. A _____ is a person who believes in the teachings of Buddha.

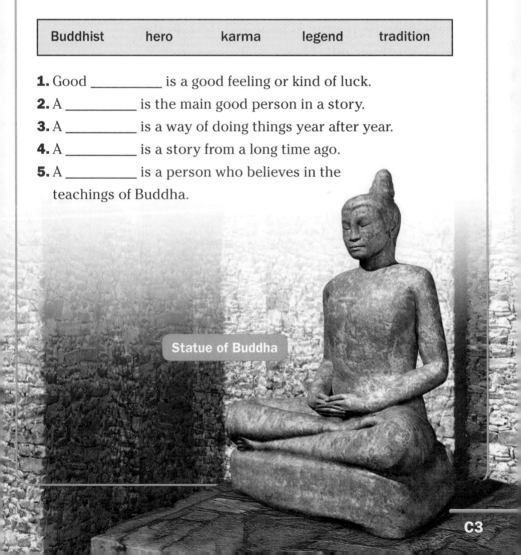

Statue of Buddha

In the town of Lopburi, Thailand, there are monkeys everywhere. They run around the streets. They climb on cars, houses, and other buildings. They can go anywhere they want to, and they get into everything!

The monkeys in this town are very playful and sometimes they cause a lot of trouble. But what about the people of Lopburi? How do they feel about these **mischievous**[1] little animals?

---

[1]**mischievous:** playful in a partly bad way; troublesome

 CD 1, Track 05

C5

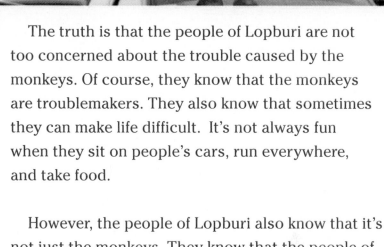

The truth is that the people of Lopburi are not too concerned about the trouble caused by the monkeys. Of course, they know that the monkeys are troublemakers. They also know that sometimes they can make life difficult. It's not always fun when they sit on people's cars, run everywhere, and take food.

However, the people of Lopburi also know that it's not just the monkeys. They know that the people of the town also cause part of the problem. They allow the monkeys to run around the streets. They allow them to cause trouble. They don't try to stop the monkeys. And once a year, the people of Lopburi do even more. They have a monkey party! They have a banquet with lots of food—for the monkeys!

But why do they have this big monkey party? Why do they present the monkeys with a banquet? The reason involves legend and tradition. Most people in Thailand are Buddhists, and for many of them monkeys are very important animals. Monkeys appear in many Thai stories and legends. Because of one special story, some Thai people consider monkeys to be heroes.

In Thailand, there is a famous old legend about a monkey hero named **Hanuman**.[2] In the story, a **demon**[3] takes the god Rama's wife. The monkey Hanuman helps to save Rama's wife. Because of this, Hanuman becomes a hero.

---

[2]**Hanuman:** (hʌnʊmɑn)
[3]**demon:** a bad spirit

Hanuman

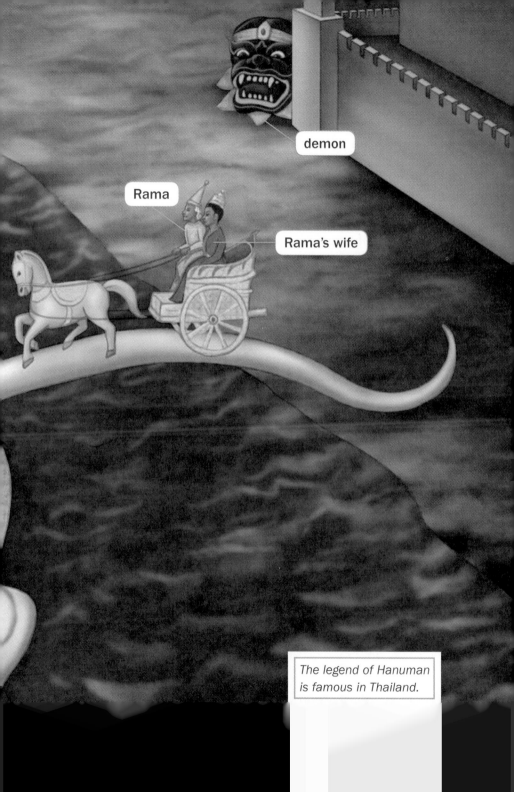

demon

Rama

Rama's wife

The legend of Hanuman is famous in Thailand.

Due to the legend of Hanuman and Buddhist traditions, many people in Thailand are still especially kind to monkeys today. This kindness is not limited to allowing monkeys to do anything they wish. Monkeys also get special food often—not just at festivals.

Every day of the year, people bring food for the monkeys to shrines. These people think it's good karma to give them food. The people also think that it will bring them good luck. With this special treatment, the monkeys of Lopburi are getting bigger and bigger all the time!

Fact Check

1. Why do Thai Buddhists like monkeys?

2. What do Thai people do because they like the monkeys?

3. What's happening to the monkeys because of this?

The time for the yearly monkey party finally arrives. It's a time when the community of Lopburi can show the monkeys just how much they like them. They always give the monkeys a lot of special foods at this time. But this year there's a particularly special treat. The festival organizers are giving the monkeys a whole cake!

An organizer of the event explains the banquet and the Buddhist traditions. He says: "Every year there are a lot of people who come and help with the monkey banquet. We want people to help offer food to the monkeys. This is because these monkeys are part of our local Buddhist tradition."

What about this year's cake? Well, it's a very big one, and a lot of people help to make it. The festival organizer explains: "This year, we've made a cake that is **four meters**[4] long for the monkey banquet. Fifty people worked to make this cake. We all wanted to find out if the monkeys liked the cake." Will the monkeys like the cake? Will they want to eat it all?

---

[4] **four meters:** 13.12 feet

MONKEY PARTY FESTIVAL

งานเลี้ยงโต๊ะจีนลิง ครั้งที่

Scan for Information

Scan pages C16 and C17 to answer
these questions.

1. Do many people want to help make
   the cake?

2. How long is the cake?

3. How many people worked to make
   the cake?

At last, the festival organizers give the monkeys the cake. They don't just like the cake, they love it! The people of Lopburi are very happy and this year's Monkey Party is a big success.

Maybe the people of Lopburi will get good karma because they've treated the monkeys well and given them this beautiful cake. Maybe they won't. Either way, the people of this Thai town did learn one thing—if you want to have a great party for monkeys, give them cake!

C19

After You Read

1. In Lopburi, mischievous monkeys are _____.
   A. anything
   B. everywhere
   C. anywhere
   D. everything

2. Which is NOT a reason why the monkeys are troublemakers?
   A. They sit on cars.
   B. They are heroes.
   C. They get into everything.
   D. They take food.

3. Why are people part of the monkey problem?
   A. because they worry too much
   B. because they make life difficult
   C. because they know that the monkeys cause trouble
   D. because they allow the monkeys to be mischievous

4. How many times in one year do people in Lopburi have a monkey banquet?
   A. three
   B. two
   C. one
   D. doesn't say

5. On page C10, 'this' refers to:
   A. saving Rama's wife
   B. being a monkey
   C. being a demon
   D. the legend

6. What is a good heading for page C10?
   A. The Legend of the Fat Monkey
   B. Monkey Hero Saves Rama's Wife
   C. Monkeys Make Life Difficult
   D. Thailand's Important Party

7. On page C12, the writer's purpose is:
   A. to teach a legend about a monkey
   B. to show why people are nice to the monkeys
   C. to explain why monkeys like cake
   D. to show that the monkeys are getting smaller

8. Some Buddhist people give food to monkeys because they believe each of these EXCEPT:
   A. the legend of Hanuman
   B. the monkeys are special
   C. it's good karma
   D. the monkeys are too big

9. Why do the festival organizers like the monkeys?
   A. because they eat cake
   B. because they are part of tradition
   C. because the party is fun
   D. because many people come

10. _____ people come to help make the cake for the monkey banquet.
   A. No
   B. A lot of
   C. Much
   D. One hundred

11. On page C18, the word 'thing' means:
   A. word
   B. piece of information
   C. way to make a cake
   D. legend

The Jataka Stories
of Buddha

Thai Buddhists follow the teachings of Buddha. Four hundred years after Buddha died, someone wrote down some of his stories in stone. These stories are called the 'Jataka Stories.' The Jataka Stories had a very important function in the past. Buddhists used them to show people how to lead a good life. These traditional stories are now legends in Thailand. The heroes in a lot of these stories are monkeys. One well-known Jataka Story features a monkey, a crocodile, and a river.

The Jataka Stories

river bank

crocodile

river

A long time ago, a monkey lived alone on a river bank. He was a very strong monkey. In the center of the river there was a small area of land. On this land there was a lovely garden with trees that provided food for the monkey. There was also a large stone halfway between the river bank and the garden. Although it seemed impossible, every day the monkey stepped from the river bank onto the stone. Then he stepped from the stone to the garden. He did this to collect food from the trees in the garden.

One day, the monkey was in the garden and a crocodile laid down on the stone. The crocodile wanted to catch the monkey and eat him. At first the monkey wasn't aware of the crocodile. But then he looked closely at the stone and realized that it was different. "Hello, Mr. Stone. How are you?" said the monkey. The crocodile quickly answered without thinking, "I'm fine. I'm going to eat you." Then the monkey said, "Very well. Open your mouth." The crocodile had to close his eyes when he opened his mouth. So the monkey carefully stepped on his head and then safely onto the river bank. The crocodile lost his dinner that day. The lesson of the story is: always take time to think carefully before you answer a question.

CD 1, Track 06

Word Count: 316
Time: _____

Vocabulary List

banquet (C: 2, 7, 8, 16, 18)
cake (C: 2, 15, 16, 18)
demon (C: 10, 11)
festival (C: 2, 12, 15, 16, 18)
four meters (C: 16)
hero (C: 3, 8, 10)
karma (C: 3, 12, 18)
legend (C: 3, 8, 10, 11, 12)
mischievous (C: 4)
monkey (C: 2, 3, 4, 7, 8, 10, 12, 13, 15, 16, 18)
shrine (C: 2, 12)
tradition (C: 3, 8, 12, 16)

The Future of
a Village

Rob Waring, *Series Editor*

HEINLE
CENGAGE Learning™

Australia • Brazil • Japan • Korea • Mexico • Singapore • Spain • United Kingdom • United States

Words to Know

This story is set in Northwest Africa. It happens in Morocco, in the village of Essaouira [ɛsəwɪərə].

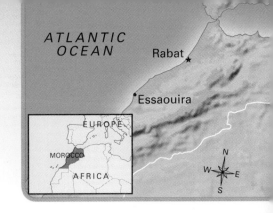

ATLANTIC OCEAN

Rabat

Essaouira

EUROPE

MOROCCO

AFRICA

N W E S

 A Fishing Village. Read the paragraph. Label the items in the picture with the <u>underlined</u> words. Then answer the questions.

Essaouira is a very old <u>village</u> near the Atlantic Ocean. It's a fishing **port** and many of the local people are <u>fishermen</u>. Most fishermen go out in a small <u>fishing boat</u> every day. They catch <u>fish</u> and sell them. Fishing has always been important in Essaouira. However, today fishing and <u>boat building</u> are not the only businesses here. Groups of **tourists** are also coming to this interesting village. They come to enjoy the town and its history—and spend money.

1. Which definition best describes '**port**'?
   a. a place by the sea where boats arrive and leave
   b. an area far out in the ocean

2. Which definition best describes '**tourists**'?
   a. visitors who go to see interesting places
   b. a kind of fisherman

B A Tourist Center. Complete the paragraph with the words in the box. Then answer the questions.

culture	environment	pollution	tourism

(1) _____ is the business of bringing visitors to an area. However, both benefits and problems come with tourists. Tourism can affect the (2) _____, or nature, of a place. It can increase (3) _____ by making the area unclean and noisy. Tourism can also affect the (4) _____ of a group of people. It can make them forget their traditions and history.

1. What are some of the benefits of tourism? _____

2. What are some of the problems with tourism? _____

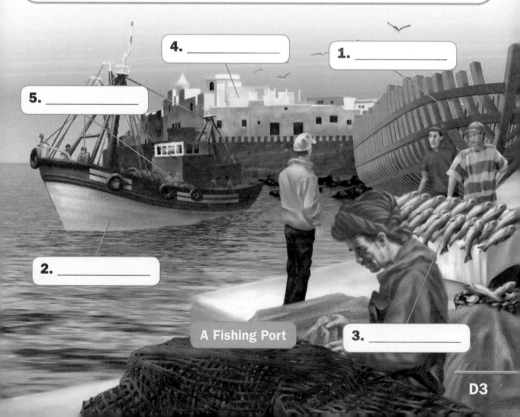

4. _____

1. _____

5. _____

2. _____

A Fishing Port

3. _____

Essaouira's fishermen are preparing for another year out on the waters of the Atlantic Ocean. All around this port in Morocco, you can hear the sounds of boat building and smell **fresh**[1] paint in the air. Everything seems great in Essaouira. It looks like the fishing business is good.

---

[1]**fresh:** new

🎧 CD 1, Track 07

But in reality, things are not very good here. In Essaouira, fishing is no longer such a good job. The number of fish that the fishermen catch has gone down in recent years. Some of the fishing work has gone away; it's moved to the south of Morocco. The size of the boats is one of the biggest problems. The small boats which leave this port can't **compete with**[2] the big fishing boats from other places. Those big boats, or trawlers, can simply catch more fish.

One fisherman explains the difficulties of life as a fisherman in Essaouira. He says that there's not a lot of work, and sometimes there's no work at all: "The life of a fisherman now is hard," he says. "Sometimes you work for one day; then you don't work for two days. Then you work for one week; then no work for fifteen days." The fishing industry here is trying to **survive**,[3] but it's very difficult. However, now there's new hope for the town of Essaouira.

---

[2] **compete with:** try to do better than
[3] **survive:** continue to exist

Recently, this town has found a new **breadwinner**;[4] tourism. Many people think that this breadwinner will be the future of Essaouira.

Last year, thousands of tourists visited Essaouira from all over the world. This tourism has brought hope and money to the town. Can tourism bring more money to the village than fishing? Does it hold the future of this old fishing village?

---

[4] **breadwinner:** main person or business that makes money

For now, no one can be certain. However, tourism is not new here. Essaouira's first **tourist boom**[5] was in the 1960s. Rock stars and people from many different cultures visited the village. They wanted to walk in its little streets, see the port and enjoy its beauty. But then tourism went away and the people had to depend more on fishing again.

Now, the small town is trying to bring in tourists again. The people of Essaouira worry that perhaps the fishing industry is dying. They want a different way to make money, perhaps an easier way. Their plan is working well—tourism is growing fast here. Since 1996, tourism in Essaouira has increased by more than three hundred percent!

---

[5]**tourist boom:** successful time for tourist businesses

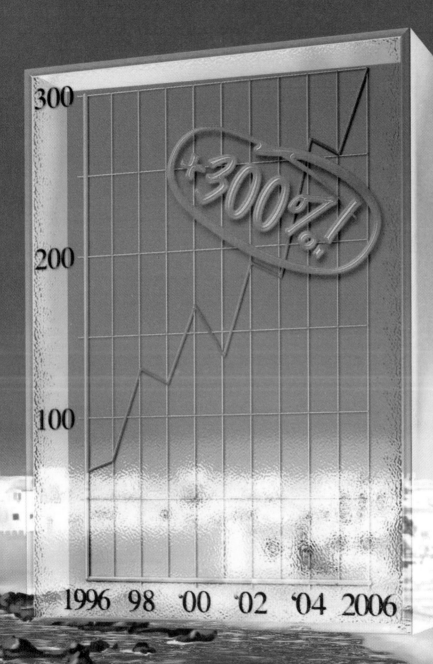

D11

D12

It's not difficult to see why visitors like the village. It's very beautiful, and it's also very old. There's also a lot of history there. Essaouira's 'medina,' or old town center, was built in the 1700s. It was recently put on **UNESCO's World Heritage List**[6]. It's a place where visitors can go back in time to a different world.

---

[6]**UNESCO World Heritage List:** a list of important cultural places in the world chosen by the United Nations Educational, Scientific, and Cultural Organization (UNESCO)

Essaouira now has a very good chance to develop tourism and help its economy. However tourism can also bring changes and problems with it. Sometimes, when tourism increases, the economy grows too quickly. This can cause problems for the local culture. The local environment can become worse because of pollution, as well.

It's going to be important for this village not to **sell out**[7] its people, culture, and environment. It's also going to be important that the tourist industry doesn't grow too quickly.

---

[7]**sell out:** give away something valuable for money (negative meaning)

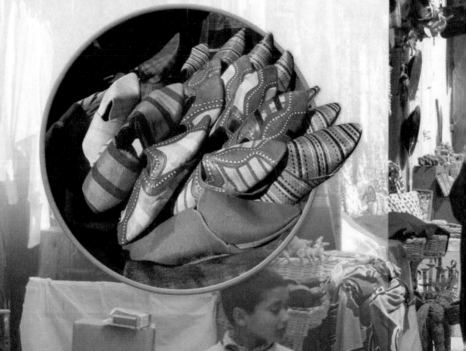

SOLDE

D15

The people who are developing tourism in Essaouira say that **conservation**[8] is very important to them. However, for the people of the village there are still questions about water, land use, and pollution. They want a business that makes money, but they also know that they have to be very careful. They know that they can't allow tourism to grow without some control.

---

[8]**conservation:** keeping the environment clean

What do you think?

1. Should Essaouira increase tourism?

2. Why or why not?

3. What should they do to keep their culture and traditions safe?

D17

D18

Is fishing now part of Essaouira's past? Maybe. Perhaps now this quiet fishing port has a chance to make a new life for itself; a life for the future.

The people of Essaouira now have to make some very important decisions. Will they be able to control the pollution? Will they be able to save the environment? Will they choose well? No one knows. The people of Essaouira do know one thing; what they do now is important. The future of their beautiful little village for tomorrow, may depend on the decisions they make today.

After You Read

1. The word 'great' on page D4 can be replaced by:
   A. enjoy
   B. noisy
   C. busy
   D. fine

2. Each is a problem for the fishermen of Essaouira EXCEPT:
   A. Their boats are too small.
   B. There are too few fish.
   C. They are getting ready.
   D. They can't compete with trawlers.

3. Sometimes fishermen don't have _____ work for fifteen days.
   A. any
   B. no
   C. one
   D. a

4. What is a good heading for page D10?
   A. Rock Star Coming to Essaouira
   B. Tourism Brings Hope and Money
   C. Morocco Loves Essaouira
   D. Too Many Tourists

5. In paragraph 2 on page D10, 'they' refers to:
   A. people from different cultures
   B. tourists in Essaouira
   C. rock stars
   D. the people of Essaouira

6. According to the paragraph on page D13 Essaouira is a _____ and _____ town.
   A. beautiful, historic
   B. different, historic
   C. famous, medina
   D. great, safe

7. What does 'it' refer to in 'it was recently' on page D13?
   A. tourism
   B. the medina
   C. Essaouira
   D. UNESCO

8. What is one reason Essaouira has a good chance to develop tourism?
   A. People are interested in the old town center.
   B. The environment is not safe.
   C. Tourists can meet fishermen.
   D. The small boats are good for tourists.

9. The best heading for page D16 is:
   A. Tourism Helps Local Culture
   B. Water Pollution
   C. Conservation Begins with Tourism
   D. Tourism without Control May Be Bad

10. What does 'past' mean on page D19?
    A. story
    B. history
    C. environment
    D. tourism

11. What is the purpose of this story?
    A. to show that fishermen have problems
    B. to teach that tourism is good
    C. to teach that conservation is important
    D. to tell about an old town trying to make a new life

What's happening to Maui?

Hawaii is a collection of six small islands near the center of the Pacific Ocean. It is almost always warm in Hawaii, so millions of tourists visit the islands each year. All of the islands are beautiful, but Maui is especially beautiful. As a result, it is one of the tourists' favorite places to visit. This island alone receives more than two million tourists every year.

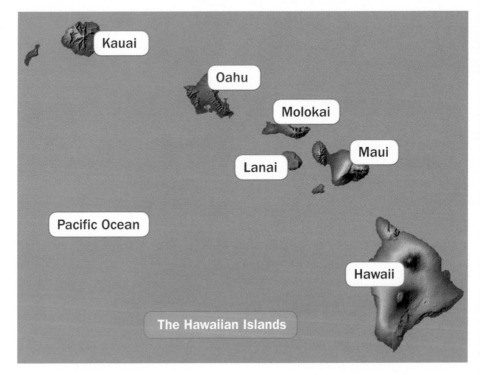

Kauai

Oahu

Molokai

Maui

Lanai

Pacific Ocean

Hawaii

The Hawaiian Islands

For many years, the main business and form of trade in Maui was farming. However, a tourist boom began in the 1960s. Since then, tourism has become the most important industry on the island.

sand

ocean

beach

The sand on Maui's beaches can be different colors.

Most tourists visit Maui because of the beaches. They are especially interesting because the sand in some places is white and in other places it can seem to be black, red, or even green.

Unfortunately, Maui's travel industry does have some serious problems. First of all, the two million tourists who visit the island each year need somewhere to stay. Therefore, land developers have built many large buildings in some of the most beautiful areas. Many of them are not very nice to look at. The buildings have also had a bad effect on the environment and there has been an increase in air and water pollution. Conservation groups have tried, but they are not able to slow this growth.

In addition, tourists need people to care for them. Therefore, more people are now living on the island all year round. In the 1960s, the number of people living on Maui was about 40,000. Today it is almost 140,000!

The traditional Hawaiian culture is now no longer easy to find. Some old villages no longer exist. The people of Maui must make some important decisions for their future. They must decide how to save their island and keep tourists happy at the same time.

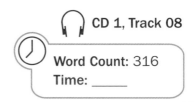

CD 1, Track 08

Word Count: 316
Time: _____

Vocabulary List

boat building (D: 2, 4)
boom (D: 7, 10)
breadwinner (D: 7, 9)
compete with (D: 6)
conservation (D: 16)
culture (D: 3, 10, 14, 16)
environment (D: 3, 14, 19)
fish (D: 2, 6)
fishermen (D: 2, 4, 6)
fishing boat (D: 2, 6)
fresh (D: 4)
pollution (D: 3, 14, 16, 19)
port (D: 2, 3, 4, 6, 10, 19)
sell out (D: 14)
survive (D: 6)
tourism (D: 3, 9, 10, 14, 16)
tourist (D: 2, 9, 10)
village (D: 2, 9, 10, 13, 14, 16, 19)

Life on the
ORINOCO

Rob Waring, *Series Editor*

HEINLE
CENGAGE Learning™

Australia • Brazil • Japan • Korea • Mexico • Singapore • Spain • United Kingdom • United States

Words to Know

This story is set in South America. It starts near Brazil and goes through the country of Venezuela. It happens on the Orinoco [ɔrɪnoʊkoʊ] River.

A **Landscapes of the Orinoco.** Read the definitions and look at the picture below. Write the number of the correct <u>underlined</u> word next to each item.

1. The <u>ocean</u> is a very large body of water; a sea.
2. A <u>delta</u> is the place where a big river enters the sea.
3. <u>Mountains</u> are very high areas of land.
4. A large area of flat land is called a <u>plain</u>.
5. A <u>waterfall</u> is a place where water is falling from a higher area.
6. A <u>river</u> is a large body of water that moves in one direction.
7. A <u>stream</u> is a small body of water that moves in one direction.
8. A <u>rain</u> <u>forest</u> is a large area of trees and other plants where it rains every day.

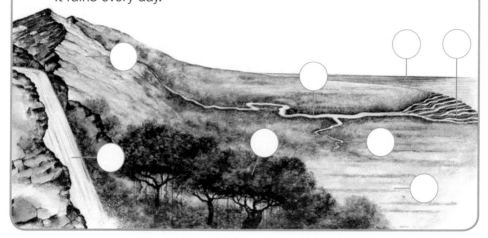

B **Animals of the Orinoco.** Here are some wild animals you will find in the story. Label the picture with the words in the box.

anaconda
capybara [kæpɪbeɪrə]
crocodile
jaguar
piranha [pɪrɑnyə]

1. _____

4. _____

2. _____

3. _____

5. _____

The Orinoco River in South America is one of the longest rivers in the world. It starts in the mountains of Venezuela and Brazil. It then **flows**[1] for nearly **1,300 miles**[2] to its delta on the Atlantic Ocean.

On its way north, the Orinoco flows through many different landscapes. It moves past **ancient**[3] stone formations, over waterfalls, through rain forest areas, and across large plains.

---

[1] **flow:** move forward; usually continuously and easily
[2] **1,300 miles:** 2,092 kilometers
[3] **ancient:** very old

CD 1, Track 09

The Orinoco Delta is the area where the river's water flows into the ocean. The area around the delta is full of streams and small waterways. These smaller rivers, or tributaries, connect to the larger Orinoco. One of these tributaries, called the **Caroni**,[4] features Angel Falls. Angel Falls is the highest waterfall in the world!

---

[4] **Caroni:** [kɑrəni]

Angel Falls, which is on an Orinoco tributary, is the highest waterfall in the world.

However, there's more than just water in the delta. The Orinoco Delta is also home to several South American Indian cultures. They have lived next to the river for thousands of years and they still live there today. Actually, the name 'Orinoco' comes from a local language. It means 'place to **paddle**'. [5]

One of these Orinoco Indian cultures is the **Yanomami**. [6] About two thousand Yanomami people live near the river, far from the rest of the world. For them, and about twenty other local cultures, the Orinoco is an important **natural resource**. [7] The river not only gives them a means of travel, but also a supply of clean water and food. The Orinoco River greatly supports these traditional cultures.

---

[5] **paddle:** move a small boat through water with a short piece of flat wood
[6] **Yanomami:** [yænəmɑmi]
[7] **natural resource:** things which naturally exist in a place and can be used by people

a waterway

a paddle

The rain forest around the Orinoco River has many kinds of plants and animals. It is home to more than a thousand different types of birds. In the river itself, there are many types of fish—including the dangerous piranha! And on the land around the river, you'll find even more interesting animals …

... like the Orinoco crocodile. He may have a big smile, but be careful! These animals can grow to more than **18 feet**[8] long! This makes the Orinoco crocodile one of the longest crocodiles in the world.

There are big snakes on the Orinoco River too. One of the biggest is the anaconda. It's one of the largest kinds of snakes in the world.

In the rain forest, you may have a chance to see one of the area's beautiful jaguars. But on the open plains, you will more likely see a totally different animal—the world's biggest **rodent**,[9] the capybara.

---

[8]**18 feet:** 6.10 meters
[9]**rodent:** a kind of small animal with long, sharp teeth

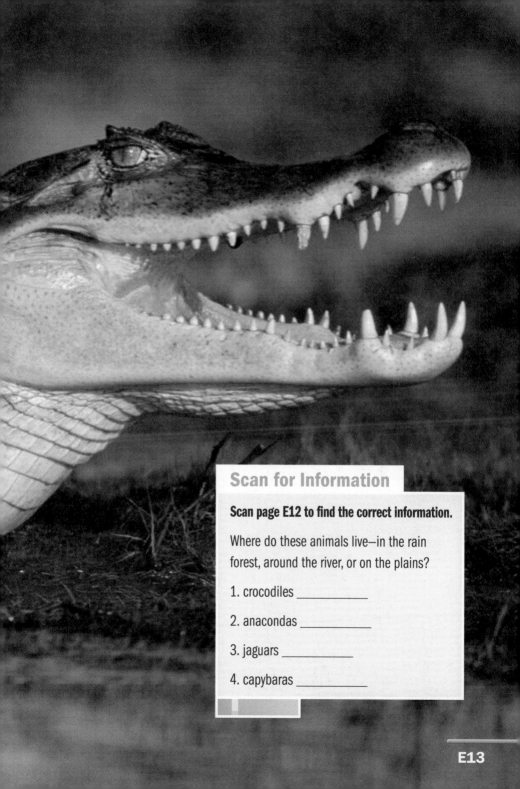

Scan for Information

Scan page E12 to find the correct information.

Where do these animals live—in the rain forest, around the river, or on the plains?

1. crocodiles _____

2. anacondas _____

3. jaguars _____

4. capybaras _____

E14

However, over the past fifty years, things have changed along the Orinoco River. Some of the cities and towns have grown significantly. These cities have also taken some of the land where animals and plants once were. The new industrial world is slowly coming to the Orinoco Delta. But what industries have been introduced? More importantly, what are they doing to the beautiful river, its animals, and its people?

Identify the Main Idea

1. What is the main idea of the paragraph on page E15?

2. What are two pieces of information that support this idea?

One of the industries that has grown is electricity production. Parts of the Orinoco now have **dams**[10] to help control the water. These dams also collect the river's water to create electrical power.

There are also other industries in the area as well. Companies there have found valuable products, like **gold**,[11] **diamonds**,[12] and **oil**.[13] Very big ships now travel up and down the river from the Atlantic Ocean to move these products.

---

[10] **dam:** a strong wall built across a river to stop the water
[11] **gold:** a valuable, shiny, yellow metal
[12] **diamonds:** very valuable clear stones
[13] **oil:** a thick black liquid that comes from under the ground

a dam

gold

diamonds

oil

a ship

It's clear that there have been some big changes on the Orinoco in recent years. But not everything has changed. Many sections of the river and the areas around them have stayed almost the same. The people of Venezuela want to continue to enjoy the river's beauty and animals.

There are now several national parks and rain forest **preserves**[14] in the delta. These parks and preserves will help this great river remain an important natural resource for Venezuela. For now, the great Orinoco River is safe. It can continue to support the birds, animals, and people that depend on it.

---

[14] **preserve:** an area of land used to protect wild plants and animals

E19

After You Read

1. The Orinoco River flows _____ the mountains _____ the sea.
   A. under, into
   B. down, from
   C. from, to
   D. to, and

2. A good heading for page E8 is:
   A. Water Is Area for Travel Only
   B. Orinoco Used for Hundreds of Years
   C. Orinoco Only Helps Yanomami Culture
   D. River Is Important to Local Cultures

3. What does the writer think about the rain forest?
   A. It's always dangerous.
   B. It's varied and interesting.
   C. It's safe to swim there.
   D. It's a quiet place.

4. Why is the jaguar special?
   A. It is the biggest rodent.
   B. It is the longest animal.
   C. It is a large type of snake.
   D. none of the above

5. In paragraph 2, on page E12, 'it' refers to the:
   A. crocodile
   B. capybara
   C. anaconda
   D. jaguar

6. On page E15, the phrase 'have grown significantly' can be replaced by:
   A. have grown a lot
   B. have not really grown
   C. have reduced in size
   D. have stayed the same

7. In the last fifty years, _____ cities and towns have gotten bigger.
   A. some
   B. all
   C. no
   D. almost all

8. The cities and towns along the delta show that the area is:
   A. totally natural
   B. changing
   C. staying the same
   D. very quiet

9. Which is NOT a sign of industry?
   A. river water
   B. electricity
   C. companies
   D. big ships

10. Why are rain forest preserves necessary in the Orinoco area?
   A. to allow people to build more
   B. to develop towns
   C. to protect the natural areas
   D. to help the companies

11. The Orinoco must continue to _____ people and animals near it.
   A. enjoy
   B. help
   C. depend on
   D. support

'Exploring Our World'

an interview with Dr. Bernard Thompson

Judy: Hello. This is Judy Jamison here with our weekly science program, 'Exploring Our World.' Here to talk with us this week is the well-known scientist, Dr. Bernard Thompson. In 2007, Dr. Thompson spent a year in the Amazon Rain Forest studying the local plant and animal life. Welcome, Dr. Thompson!

Dr. Thompson: Thank you, Judy. I'm happy to be here.

Judy: So, can you tell us a little about your work?

Dr. Thompson: Certainly! I'm interested in helping protect all forms of life in the forest. This includes everything from the beautiful jaguars on the land, to the piranhas in the rivers. We also want to protect their environment as well. We want to save the trees that make up the rain forest and keep the rivers clean.

Judy: And what did you learn on your latest trip?

The Amazon Rain Forest covers a large part of South America.

Rain Forest area

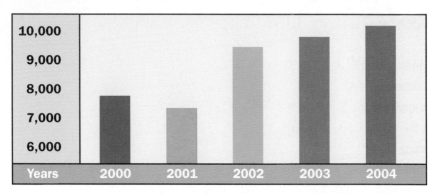

Square Miles of Rain Forest Lost Each Year

Dr. Thompson:	Unfortunately, I learned some things that really worried me. Did you know the rain forest is becoming smaller and smaller every year? Data shows that in the year 2000, the area lost about 7,500 square miles of forest. In 2004, we lost over 10,000 square miles!
Judy:	What are the causes of this?
Dr. Thompson:	Some large companies are cutting down a lot of the trees. They want to get to the natural resources in the area. Some are looking for oil. Others are looking for gold and diamonds. Farmers are also clearing a lot of the land. Wood from the trees has also become a valuable product all over the world. It's a big problem!
Judy:	Yes, it sounds serious.
Dr. Thompson:	It is. And in order to help people get these valuable resources, some governments are building roads. These roads are bringing more people and machines to the area. This means that the rain forest will continue to be cut down quickly.
Judy:	What will happen if the current situation doesn't change?
Dr. Thompson:	Well, according to recent theories, the rain forest could be gone within 30 years …

CD 1, Track 10

Word Count: 324

Time: _____

Vocabulary List

anaconda (E: 3, 12, 13)
ancient (E: 4)
capybara (E: 3, 12, 13)
crocodile (E: 3, 12, 13)
dam (E: 16)
delta (E: 2, 4, 7, 8, 15, 18)
diamond (E: 16, 17)
flow (E: 4, 7, 8)
gold (E: 16, 17)
jaguar (E: 3, 12, 13, 14)
mountain (E: 2, 4)
natural resource (E: 8, 18)
ocean (E: 2, 4, 7, 16)
oil (E: 16, 17)
paddle (E: 8, 9)
piranha (E: 3, 11)
plains (E: 2, 4, 12, 13)
preserve (E: 18)
rain forest (E: 2, 4, 11, 12, 13, 18)
river (E: 2, 4, 7, 8, 11, 12, 13, 15, 16, 18)
rodent (E: 12)
stream (E: 2, 7)
waterfall (E: 2, 4, 7)

The Lost City of
Machu Picchu

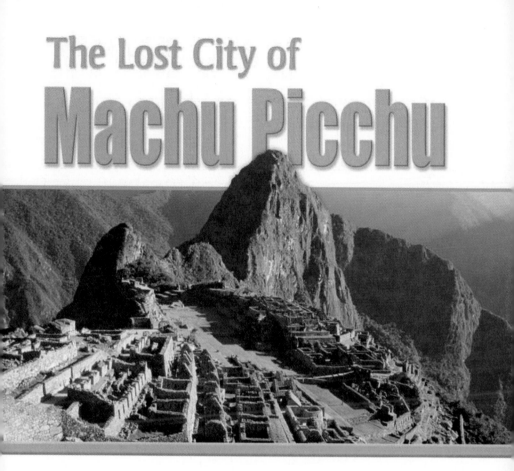

Rob Waring, *Series Editor*

HEINLE
CENGAGE Learning

Australia • Brazil • Japan • Korea • Mexico • Singapore • Spain • United Kingdom • United States

Words to Know

This story is set in Peru, South America. It happens at a place called Machu Picchu [mɑtʃu pɪktʃu], in the Andes mountain range.

A **Machu Picchu and the Ancient World.** Read the paragraph. Complete the definitions with the underlined words.

Machu Picchu was an <u>ancient</u> city in the Andes Mountains. A group of people called the Inca built Machu Picchu a long time ago. The Inca <u>civilization</u> lasted from around A.D. 1100 until about A.D. 1500. When it suddenly ended, few people knew about Machu Picchu. Because of this, it is sometimes called the 'Lost City of the Inca.' In 1911, an American <u>explorer</u> found Machu Picchu. Since then, many people have visited Machu Picchu to <u>climb</u> the <u>ruins</u> of the city.

1. move up or over something: _____
2. very old: _____
3. a person who travels to learn about new places: _____
4. the remains of buildings: _____
5. people and culture: _____

mountains

Inca man

Inca woman

The Lost City of Machu Picchu

B **Machu Picchu and the Modern World.** Read the paragraph and notice the underlined words. Then answer the questions.

The modern world, or the world of today, has now come to Machu Picchu. A big part of this modern world is tourism. Tourism is a business that brings visitors to a place. These visitors, or tourists, come from many countries. Some conservationists think tourism might be bad for the environment. They want to protect Machu Picchu. They don't want a lot of tourists to go there.

1. Why do you think tourists want to go to modern day Machu Picchu? List three or more reasons.
2. Why do you think conservationists are worried about Machu Picchu? List three or more reasons.
3. What do you think will happen to Machu Picchu in the future? How can people protect it?

Tourists in Modern Day Machu Picchu

This beautiful, quiet place is covered in sunshine and has very high mountains all around it. Its name is Machu Picchu. It's sometimes called the 'Lost City of the Inca,' and it's nearly **8,000 feet**[1] up in the Andes Mountains of Peru.

The story of Machu Picchu is the story of a place where the ancient world and the modern world meet.

---

[1]**8,000 feet:** 2,438 meters

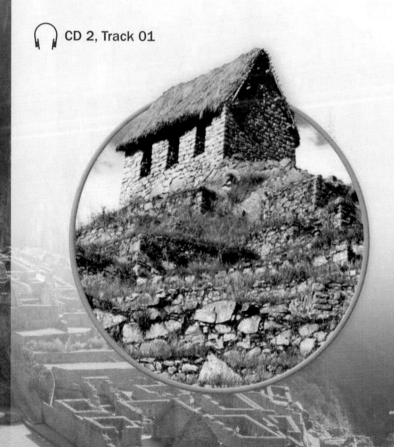

CD 2, Track 01

Julio is a **tour guide**[2] and he knows Machu Picchu very well. He thinks that it has a special quality. It has something which brings people to it. "It's a magic attraction that you can feel here," he explains. "It's known all over the world that Machu Picchu is one of the **magnetic centers**[3] of the ancient world," he says.

---

[2]**tour guide:** a person who shows visitors around and gives them information about a place

[3]**magnetic center:** a special area which pulls energy towards it

Machu Picchu is a city with a long history; it's more than 500 years old. Today, it's a favorite place for visitors. These visitors are not only people from Peru. People from all over the world go to Machu Picchu. They want to attempt to step back in time and to understand the Inca civilization. They don't only go there in the sunshine, either. Even in the **fog**,[4] many think it's wonderful to climb up the mountain and walk through the ruins of the city.

---

[4]**fog:** a cloud near the ground that makes it difficult to see

Scan for Information

Scan page F8 to find the information.

1. How old is Machu Picchu?

2. Who visits Machu Picchu?

3. What is one thing visitors do there?

When the Inca civilization ended, few people knew that Machu Picchu ever existed. For a long time Machu Picchu was lost to the outside world. Then, in 1911, an explorer named Hiram Bingham found it again.

At first, very few people visited the ruins of Machu Picchu. But now, hundreds of tourists come here every day. They walk up the steps of the ancient city and climb over the ruins. Machu Picchu is no longer quiet. It's currently full of the sounds of visitors. And not everyone likes it. Some people want the tourists to come, but other people don't.

Hiram Bingham

F12

Some people in Peru hope that even more tourists will come to Machu Picchu. They think it will mean more business and money for the country. These people want to make it easier for tourists to get to Machu Picchu. They also want to establish better, more modern, tourist services. They say that tourism will improve things for Peru and its people.

However, some conservationists worry that more visitors won't be good for Machu Picchu. They say that tourism may not be good for the environment or for the old ruins. Others worry that the ancient city will change. They worry that it will lose its special quality. They think it may become just like any other place.

One man, however, is not worried about this at all. José owns a local hotel. He says that Machu Picchu and Peru need more visitors. The 'Lost City' is a very special place, he claims, and everyone should be able to see it. "Why not be like the rest of the world?" he says. "Why not **expose**[5] and show Machu Picchu to the rest of the world?" He then adds, "It's such a wonderful place, why keep it to a few?"

It's obvious that some people, like José, support tourism, and some people are against it. So what does tourism mean to Peru? The truth is that parts of Peru are very poor. The tourist trade brings a lot of money to some communities.

---

[5] **expose:** let people see

Infer Meaning

1. What's the purpose of José's comment?

2. How does José feel about tourism in Machu Picchu?

F15

F16

Aguas Calientes[6] is a good example of a tourist community. Aguas Calientes is a town that is in the area where visitors get on buses to go to the **summit**[7] of Machu Picchu. Because of this, it grew suddenly and went from nothing into a town.

Aguas Calientes has no industry except tourism. The town is just a group of **stalls**.[8] The local people here sell art and other things they have created to the visitors. The people there live completely on money from tourists. It's their only income.

[6]**Aguas Calientes:** [ɑgwɑs kɑlyɛnteɪs]
[7]**summit:** top of a mountain
[8]**stall:** a small shop with an open front or a table

What is happening to the special quality and beauty of Machu Picchu today? Tourism is certainly changing the area. But are the effects good or bad? No one can decide.

However, one thing is certain: **Time may be running out**[9] for the 'Lost City of the Inca.' This 'Lost City' is no longer lost. Tourists have found it and the modern world is coming closer to this ancient world every day. In the end, it may be the modern world that forever changes this ancient city.

---

[9]**time may be running out:** there might not be much time left

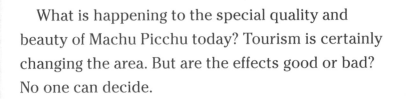

F19

After You Read

1. On page F5, the word 'beautiful' can be replaced by:
   A. sunny
   B. lovely
   C. dark
   D. hot

2. What is a good heading for page F6?
   A. People Don't Know About Machu Picchu
   B. The Magical Energy of Machu Picchu
   C. Machu Picchu Is Known All Over the Ancient World
   D. Julio Talks About the Inca

3. Machu Picchu is a city with _____ long history.
   A. the
   B. many
   C. a
   D. some

4. On page F10, 'they' in paragraph two refers to:
   A. tour guides
   B. Inca
   C. tourists
   D. explorers

5. How many visitors come to Machu Picchu every day?
   A. a few
   B. one
   C. none
   D. hundreds

6. How do conservationists feel about tourism in Macchu Picchu?
   A. If too many tourists come, the lost city will change.
   B. Many people should come to Machu Picchu.
   C. Machu Picchu is not very beautiful for tourists.
   D. The world is not interested in the lost city.

7. How does the hotel owner feel about tourism in Machu Picchu?
  A. If too many tourists come, the lost city will change.
  B. Many people should come to see Machu Picchu.
  C. Machu Picchu is not very beautiful for tourists.
  D. The world is not interested in the lost city.

8. Tourism brings _____ money to Peru.
  A. more
  B. no
  C. a
  D. the

9. On page F17, the phrase 'local people' in paragraph two means:
  A. tourists in the town
  B. people from far away
  C. people from Aguas Caliente
  D. conservationists at Machu Picchu

10. On page F18, what is 'it' in 'tourists have found it'?
  A. the modern world
  B. the special quality
  C. the ancient history
  D. the lost city

11. A good heading for page F18 is:
  A. Modern World May Bring End to Ancient City
  B. Little Time to Become a Modern City
  C. A Lot of Time Left for Machu Picchu
  D. A Modern Machu Picchu Is Better

HEINLE Times

TWO VIEWS OF MACHU PICCHU

The Heinle Times recently received two letters to the government office of tourism in Peru. One is in favor of increased tourism in the area around Machu Picchu. The other letter is against allowing large numbers of tourists to visit the ruins. You decide who's right.

Greater International Understanding

I think Peru should do everything it can to bring more tourists to Machu Picchu. People from other countries will pay a lot to visit this beautiful and historic site. I live near Machu Picchu and strongly believe this money will help the local people have a better life. Visitors from other countries also provide a way for people to share their cultures. As aresult, this will lead to greater international understanding. Bringing more attention to the area will also help people realize that it's important to keep the ruins in good condition.

Yours truly,
Richard Wellner
SBC Tours Incorporated

Not a Pleasant Experience

Recently, I visited Machu Picchu. As I reached the summit, the fog cleared and suddenly I saw the view! The mountains were so beautiful. Then our tour guide showed us some of the two hundred ancient buildings. We walked around for hours enjoying the views and looking at the buildings. It is a very special place.

However, the experience was not a totally pleasant one. I'm concerned that too many people are visiting the area. For one thing, it was impossible for us to find a quiet place to sit and enjoy the view. People were running everywhere. Secondly, I could see that the large numbers of tourists are starting to have a bad effect on the land. People have cut down a lot of the trees. They also leave paper and other things they do not want on the ground. Some of the ancient stones have even been moved or broken. I think the government should make laws limiting the number of tourists who can visit Machu Picchu each year.

Yours truly,
Martha Gorman
Concerned Community Member

CD 2, Track 02

Word Count: 339
Time: _____

Vocabulary List

ancient (F: 2, 5, 6, 10, 12, 13, 18)

civilization (F: 2, 8, 10)

climb (F: 2, 8, 10)

conservationist (F: 3, 13)

explorer (F: 2, 10)

expose (F: 14)

fog (F: 8)

magnetic center (F: 6)

modern (F: 3, 5, 13, 18)

ruins (F: 2, 8, 10, 13)

stall (F: 17)

summit (F: 17)

time may be running out (F: 18)

tour guide (F: 6)

tourism (F: 3, 14, 17, 18)

tourist (F: 3, 10, 13, 14, 17, 18)

Columbus and the New World

Rob Waring, *Series Editor*

HEINLE
CENGAGE Learning

Australia • Brazil • Japan • Korea • Mexico • Singapore • Spain • United Kingdom • United States

Words to Know

This story happens long ago. It starts in Europe, in the countries of Spain and Italy. It then goes across the Atlantic Ocean to a "new world."

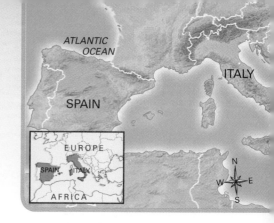

 A **The Life of Columbus.** Read the paragraph. Then match each word with the correct definition.

Christopher Columbus was a great sailor. He wanted to find a new route between Europe and Asia. At the time, some people knew that the earth was round. Columbus wanted to sail from Europe to Asia. So, he made a long voyage across the Atlantic Ocean. When he landed on a small island, Columbus thought he was in Asia. However, he was actually near a completely different continent. He was near North America. Some Europeans called this continent the 'new world' as compared to the 'old world' of Europe.

1. the earth _____

2. sail _____

3. continent _____

4. route _____

5. sailor _____

6. voyage _____

7. island _____

a. a person who sails ships as their job

b. an area of land that has water around it

c. one of the main areas of land in the world

d. the world on which we live

e. a long trip at sea

f. travel using cloth and the wind

g. the way that a person goes from one place to another

Christopher Columbus 1451–1506

B **Old World Meets New World.** Label the map with the correct countries.

the Bahamas	East Indies	Italy
China	India	Spain

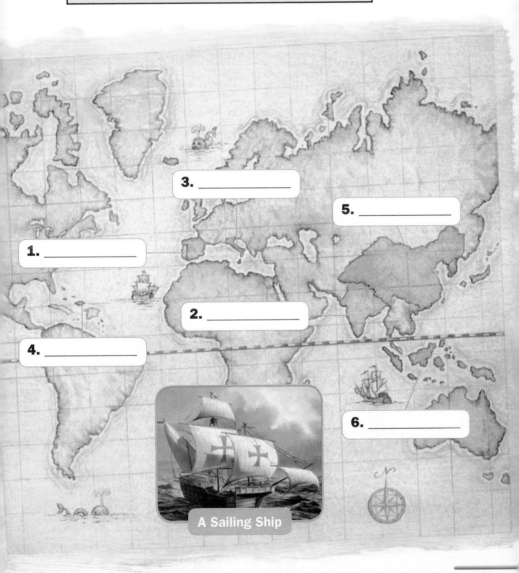

3. _____

5. _____

1. _____

2. _____

4. _____

6. _____

A Sailing Ship

Christopher Columbus was born in Italy, in 1451. The 1400s were a time of change in Europe. At that time, a lot of people in the world thought that the earth was flat. However, many educated Europeans realized that the earth was indeed round.

This possibility of a round earth changed the way that people thought. It was also of great interest to a young Columbus. When he was a young man, he decided to study **geography**.[1] He also decided to go to sea. Columbus wanted to find the answer to a major geographical problem.

---

[1]**geography:** the study of the countries of the world and the parts of the earth.

 CD 2, Track 03

G5

At the time, Europeans wanted **spices**[2] from India and China. However, it cost too much money to carry these products from the East using the traditional land and sea routes.

Columbus decided that he wanted to find a new sea route from Europe to Asia. He knew that the earth was round. Because of this, Columbus thought he could reach the East by sailing west. However, he also knew that sailing around the world would be costly. Therefore, he needed a lot of money to find out if he was right.

---

[2]**spice:** a material used to make food taste good

In 1492, Columbus **persuaded**[3] King Ferdinand and Queen Isabella of Spain to give him the money for the voyage. He received enough money for three small ships: the Nina, the Pinta, and the Santa Maria.

Columbus finally had his ships. He also had big hopes for his new sea route from Europe to Asia. Columbus and his group sailed west, but they didn't know what was waiting for them.

---

[3]**persuade:** make someone agree to do something by talking to them a lot about it

Sequence the Events

What is the correct order of the events? Number 1 to 4.

_____ Columbus received money from the King and Queen of Spain for his voyage.

_____ Columbus studied geography.

_____ Columbus sailed west.

_____ Columbus decided to find a new sea route between Europe and Asia.

G10

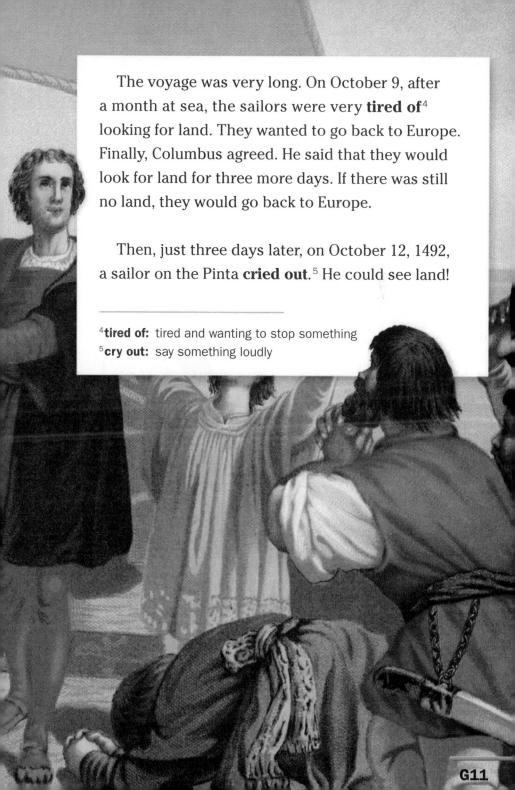

The voyage was very long. On October 9, after a month at sea, the sailors were very **tired of**[4] looking for land. They wanted to go back to Europe. Finally, Columbus agreed. He said that they would look for land for three more days. If there was still no land, they would go back to Europe.

Then, just three days later, on October 12, 1492, a sailor on the Pinta **cried out**.[5] He could see land!

---

[4]**tired of:** tired and wanting to stop something
[5]**cry out:** say something loudly

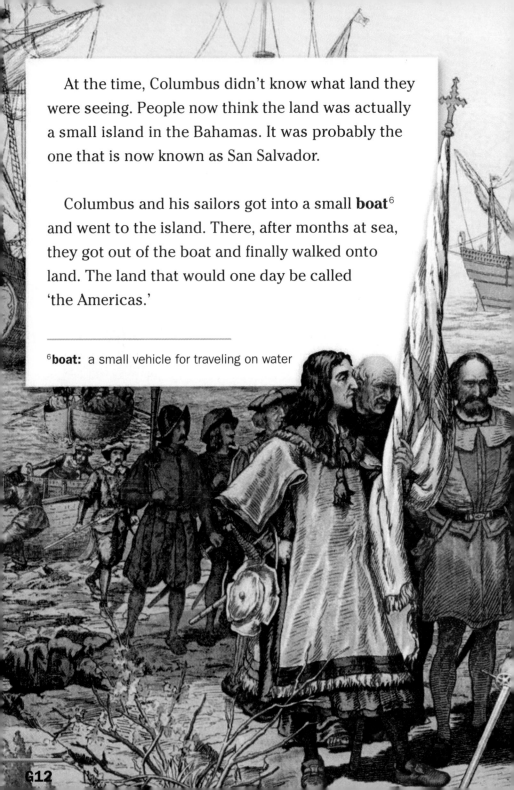

At the time, Columbus didn't know what land they were seeing. People now think the land was actually a small island in the Bahamas. It was probably the one that is now known as San Salvador.

Columbus and his sailors got into a small **boat**[6] and went to the island. There, after months at sea, they got out of the boat and finally walked onto land. The land that would one day be called 'the Americas.'

---

[6]**boat:** a small vehicle for traveling on water

However, Columbus didn't realize that he was on a new continent. He believed that he and his sailors were near the coast of Asia. He thought they were in the islands of the East Indies. He even called the island people who came to meet him 'Indians.' Because of this, people incorrectly called **Native Americans**[7] 'Indians' for hundreds of years.

Columbus returned to Spain. He brought **gold**,[8] **parrots**,[9] and other things from the New World to show the king and queen. For him, this was the high point of his life as a sailor. As a result of his voyage, he was considered by some to be a very important man in Europe.

North America

---

[7] **Native Americans:** certain groups of people who first lived in North and South America
[8] **gold:** a valuable, shiny yellow metal
[9] **parrot:** a bird from hot countries which can sometimes talk

parrot

gold

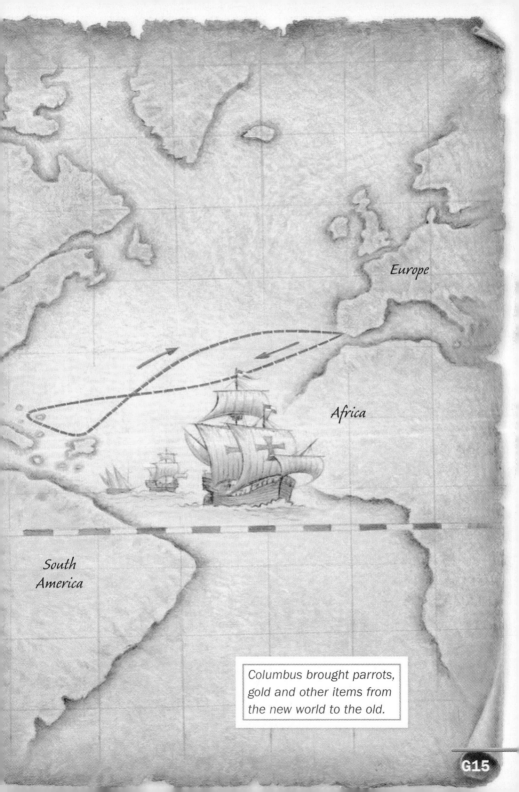

Europe

Africa

South
America

Columbus brought parrots,
gold and other items from
the new world to the old.

After his big voyage, Columbus didn't just stay in Europe. During his life, he made three more voyages to the new world. But in the end, he didn't achieve what he really wanted to do. He never found a new route to bring spices from Asia to Europe. Columbus was a **disappointed**[10] man when he died on May 20, 1506. However, questions about what Columbus achieved didn't end with his death.

---

[10] **disappointed:** unhappy because something was not as good as hoped or expected

There are still concerns about Columbus's voyage today. For hundreds of years, people believed that Columbus was the first European to reach the Americas. However, people now know that the **Vikings**[11] reached North America five hundred years earlier than Columbus did. It is true that Columbus found a new world for Europeans to **explore**.[12] However, in the end, this exploration caused a number of problems for Native Americans.

Columbus made 1492 one of the most important years in world history. However, this importance was for both good and bad reasons. One thing is certain however: on October 12, 1492, the new world—and the old—changed for all time.

---

[11] **Vikings:** groups of people from Northern Europe who traveled by sea between the 700s and 1000s
[12] **explore:** look for and find

After You Read

1. In paragraph 1 on page G4, 'educated' means:
   A. rich
   B. informed
   C. mistaken
   D. young

2. In paragraph 1 on page G7, the phrase 'these products' refers to:
   A. most people
   B. sea routes
   C. spices
   D. India and China

3. Why did Columbus want to sail west?
   A. to bring spices to Europe
   B. to answer a problem
   C. to get to the East
   D. all of the above

4. In paragraph 1 on page G11, the expression 'at sea' means:
   A. searching
   B. waiting
   C. sailing
   D. looking

5. Which is NOT a good heading for page G11?
   A. Columbus Returns to Europe
   B. Pinta Sailor Sees Land
   C. Sailors Getting Bored at Sea
   D. After Three More Days

6. Columbus sailed a small boat _____ the island.
   A. under
   B. in
   C. on
   D. to

7. Why did Columbus call the Native American people 'Indians'?
   A. They were from the East Indies.
   B. He misunderstood his location.
   C. He thought he was in India.
   D. He named them after the queen.

8. According to page G17, how many times did Columbus go to the new world in all?
   A. 4
   B. 3
   C. 2
   D. 1

9. According to page G18, how long before Columbus did the Vikings reach the new world?
   A. 1442 years
   B. 992 years
   C. 500 years
   D. 100 years

10. In paragraph 1 on page G18, the phrase 'a number of problems' can be replaced by:
   A. a lot of problems
   B. 1 or 2 problems
   C. a few problems
   D. much problems

11. What does the writer think about Columbus?
   A. He was a happy man.
   B. He did a bad thing.
   C. He did a good thing.
   D. He changed the world.

Class: Geography

Teacher: Ms. Lopez

Assignment: Write about a well-known ocean voyage. Describe the person who planned it and explain the purpose of it.

The Kon-Tiki
by Elliot Park

  When Thor Heyerdahl was a little boy, he hoped to see the world. He wanted to learn about, and visit, unusual places all over Earth. At the age of 24, he and his wife went to live on a Polynesian island in the Pacific Ocean. He became very interested in the people who lived there. He was also interested in how these people had arrived there. Most scientists believed that these people originally came from the Asian continent. However, Heyerdahl began to think that they might have come from South America. He wanted to persuade others that his idea was right. In order to do this, he decided to sail from South America to the Polynesian Islands to prove it was possible.

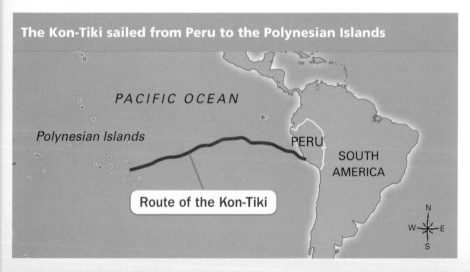

The Kon-Tiki sailed from Peru to the Polynesian Islands

PACIFIC OCEAN

Polynesian Islands

PERU

SOUTH AMERICA

Route of the Kon-Tiki

The Kon-Tiki was a large raft

Heyerdahl built a special type of boat called a 'raft.' He named it the 'Kon-Tiki.' It was the type of boat that people used to sail across the ocean centuries ago. It did not have an engine. It was made of wood and had several sails. Heyerdahl and five other men left Peru on April 28, 1947. They sailed west across the Pacific Ocean. Their voyage lasted for one hundred and one days and their route was very long. They finally arrived at the Polynesian Islands on August 7, 1947.

The voyage proved that people could sail from South America to the Polynesian Islands. However, most scientists still don't agree with Heyerdahl's idea. They don't believe that the people of Polynesia are from South America. According to them, most scientific research says differently. They argue that people from the Polynesian Islands do not have a lot in common with people from South America. They think they have more in common with people from Asia.

CD 2, Track 04

Word Count: 318
Time: _____

Vocabulary List

boat (G: 12)
continent (G: 2, 14)
cry out (G: 11)
disappointed (G: 17)
earth (G: 2, 4, 7)
explore (G: 18)
geography (G: 4, 9)
gold (G: 14)
island (G: 2, 12, 14)
parrot (G: 14)
persuade (G: 8)
route (G: 2, 7, 8, 9, 17)
sail (G: 2, 7, 8, 9)
sailor (G: 2, 11, 12, 14)
spice (G: 7, 17)
tired of (G: 11)
voyage (G: 2, 8, 9, 11, 14, 17)

Dreamtime
PAINTERS

Rob Waring, *Series Editor*

HEINLE
CENGAGE Learning™

Australia • Brazil • Japan • Korea • Mexico • Singapore • Spain • United Kingdom • United States

Words to Know

This story is set in Australia. It happens in the Kakadu [kɑkədu] National Park. A **national park** is a special area where animals and nature are protected.

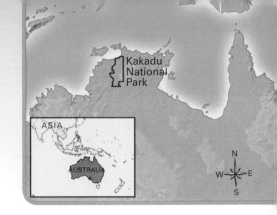

A **Animals in Australia.** Read the definitions. Write the number of the correct <u>underlined</u> word next to each item in the picture.

1. A <u>kangaroo</u> is an Australian animal that jumps on its back legs.
2. <u>Insects</u> are small living things with six legs; for example, beetles or spiders.
3. <u>Reptiles</u> are cold-blooded animals that lay eggs and have pieces of hard skin, or 'scales,' on their bodies.
4. A <u>turtle</u> is an animal with four legs and a hard back covering that lives mainly in water.
5. <u>Rock</u> is the hard, natural material that forms part of the earth.

The Australian Outback

B The Aboriginal Civilization. Read the paragraph. Then match each word with the correct definition.

The Aboriginal civilization is one of the world's most ancient civilizations. They have lived on Earth for at least forty thousand years. 'Dreamtime' is the Aboriginal story of how the world began. Aboriginal artists often paint pictures about the Dreamtime story. Aboriginal art is very beautiful and very valuable.

1. civilization _____
2. ancient _____
3. Earth _____
4. Dreamtime _____
5. artist _____
6. art _____

a. the world on which we live
b. someone who paints or draws
c. very old
d. the culture and society of a people
e. paintings and drawings
f. an Aboriginal name for the time when the world began

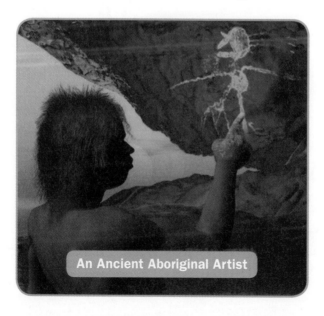

An Ancient Aboriginal Artist

Australia is a very large country with a varied landscape. It has **rain forests**,[1] the outback **desert**,[2] and the seaside. It also has a special warm area in the North. Here, you can find art that is over 30,000 years old! It is the rock art of the Dreamtime Painters.

---

[1] **rain forest:** an area with many trees and plants where it rains very often

[2] **desert:** an area, often covered with sand or rocks, that has very little water

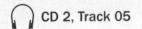 CD 2, Track 05

H5

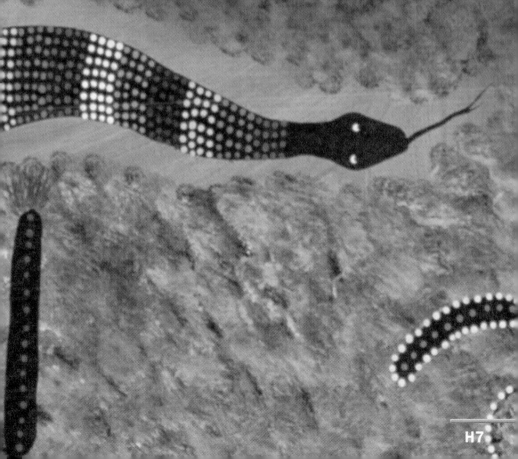

Aboriginal rock art is ancient. It was around long before there were roads and towns. It was in Australia long before people from other countries arrived. It comes from a time when Aboriginal rock artists painted the 'Dreamtime.'

Dreamtime is an Aboriginal story about the beginning of the world. It describes a time long ago when rocks, animals, plants, and people first came to the earth. It's a big part of Aboriginal history and culture.

Aboriginal images of the Dreamtime can be seen in ancient rock paintings throughout Australia. There are large numbers of these paintings under the ground of Kakadu National Park; a park which is owned by the Aboriginal people.

Rock Paintings

Ancient Dreamtime Painters made many rock paintings long ago.

Thompson Yulidgirru[3] is an Aboriginal artist. He still paints in the traditional Aboriginal way. He tells how he learned the old Aboriginal stories from his grandfather. However, the stories go back much further than Thompson's grandfather. Thompson explains, "When I used to go stay with my grandfather, I used to tell him, 'Please … tell me the stories from my **ancestors**.[4]'"

Ian Morris is a **naturalist**[5] who has lived in Australia most of his life. He has studied these Dreamtime paintings, and feels they are very special. They are unlike any other paintings in the world. Morris explains; "They say that the rock art here goes back almost as far as any known civilization. They're the oldest art records of human civilization in the world."

---

[3] **Thompson Yulidgirru:** [tɒmpsən yulɪdʒəru]
[4] **ancestor:** member of a person's family from very long ago
[5] **naturalist:** person who studies plants, animals and nature

Answer the questions. Then scan page H12
to check your answers.

1. How long have the Aboriginal people lived
   in Australia?

2. Other than the Dreamtime, what kind of
   stories do the rock paintings tell?

The Aboriginal people have most likely lived in what is now Australia for at least forty thousand years. They may have even been here for as long as a hundred thousand years. This means that they are the oldest continuous human culture on Earth.

The ancient art of the Aboriginal people is like a history book. It's also a **guide**[6] to everyday life. Their pictures tell stories about birds that tell kangaroos when **hunters**[7] are approaching. The paintings also tell stories of war.

---

[6]**guide:** a list of helpful information
[7]**hunter:** a person or an animal that kills for food or sport

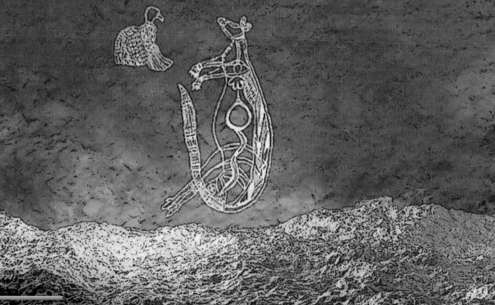

H13

H14

In the past, Aboriginal people believed that these paintings had special powers. They believed that if they painted a lot of **fish**,[8] they would catch a lot of fish. The **seasons**[9] of the year were significant to the Aboriginal people, as well. They only painted certain images at specific times of the year.

In addition, certain groups of Aboriginals only painted certain animals. If a group painted turtles, that's the only thing they painted. They didn't paint kangaroos as well. These ancient painters regarded their art as special. They thought it kept the earth strong and healthy.

---

[8]**fish:** a kind of animal that usually has scales and lives in water
[9]**season:** one of the four periods of the year; spring, summer, fall, or winter

However, things have changed nowadays. Most Aboriginal painters no longer paint on rock. In fact, the last real rock artists died in the 1960s. Today Aboriginal artists paint on **bark**,[10] paper, and wood. That way, they can carry their art everywhere and sell it easily.

Aboriginal art is getting more and more **famous**.[11] People everywhere want to buy Aboriginal art and prices are sometimes very high. One piece of Aboriginal art can now cost a lot of money, perhaps tens of thousands of Australian dollars.

---

[10]**bark:** the hard outer covering of a tree
[11]**famous:** known and recognized by many people

Fact Check: True or false?

1. There aren't any real rock artists today.

2. Artists now paint on paper and wood.

3. Aboriginal art does not cost very much.

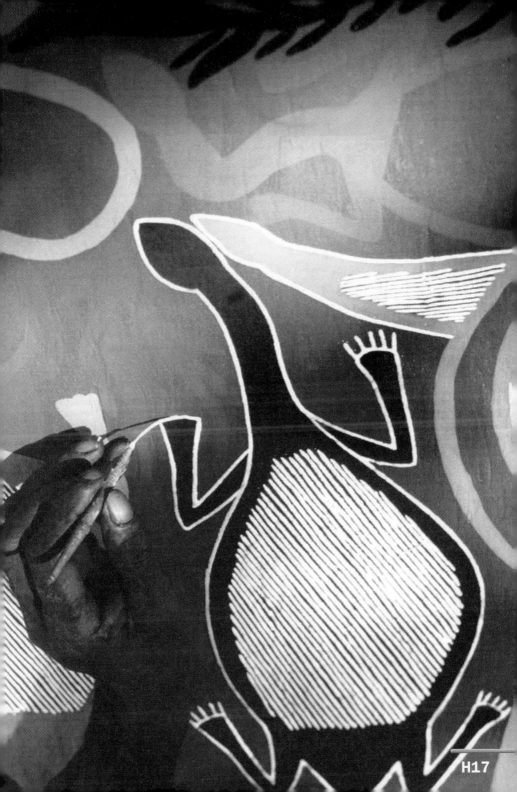

H17

Unfortunately there's now a problem with the original rock paintings. Many of them are losing their color due to time and bad weather. Insects and reptiles also walk over the paintings and make them lose their color. "There are all these **agents of deterioration**[12] acting on the art," reports Morris. "We can only slow that down [not stop it]." Fortunately, there is a lot of rock art in Australia, and they're finding more all the time.

Many Aboriginal people are trying to keep in contact with their history in modern times. The rock art of the Dreamtime Painters may just help them do this. Hopefully, these ancient paintings will help modern-day Aboriginal people understand the thoughts and ideas of their ancestors. Hopefully, they will help save the memories of the great civilizations who owned this land long ago, and who still own it today.

---

[12] **agents of deterioration:** things that make the condition of something worse

After You Read

1. On page H4, what is the meaning of the word 'varied'?
   A. simple
   B. changing
   C. artistic
   D. beautiful

2. What is the best heading for page H7?
   A. Rock Art Shows Recent Aboriginal Stories
   B. Ancient Towns and Roads in Rock Painting
   C. Dreamtime Paintings Tell of Long Ago
   D. Aboriginal Music Tells Ancient Story

3. What did the artist Thompson Yulidgirru want his grandfather to teach him about?
   A. making rock art
   B. his family's history
   C. ways to paint
   D. Aboriginal beliefs

4. Naturalist Ian Morris thinks that Aboriginal rock art:
   A. is special to the world
   B. shows that Aboriginal civilization is modern
   C. was not painted by Aboriginal people
   D. all of the above

5. The Aboriginal people have the oldest _____ in the world.
   A. continuous human culture
   B. towns
   C. naturalists
   D. painter

6. On page H15, 'significant' means:
   A. hard
   B. wonderful
   C. important
   D. troubling

7. Why do Aboriginal artists paint on bark now?
   A. There are no more rocks.
   B. They like paper and wood.
   C. It's easier to paint on bark.
   D. People can buy and move bark paintings.

8. One piece of Aboriginal art can cost:
   A. hundreds of Australian dollars
   B. thousands of Australian dollars
   C. tens of thousands of Australian dollars
   D. hundreds of thousands of Australian dollars

9. In paragraph one on page H19, 'them' refers to:
   A. paintings
   B. insects
   C. artists
   D. reptiles

10. How can we stop the deterioration of the rock paintings?
   A. Brighten the colors.
   B. Kill insects and reptiles.
   C. Stop the bad weather.
   D. There is nothing we can do.

11. People are _____ finding Aboriginal rock art all the time.
   A. many
   B. still
   C. even
   D. ever

The LASCAUX PAINTINGS

Near the town of Montignac in Southern France, visitors can find some of the most beautiful cave paintings in the world—the Lascaux Paintings. The history of these paintings is very interesting. Caves are large rooms that have been formed by nature. Most caves are under the ground, but some have entrances that people can find. In September 1940, that's just what happened. Four boys were taking a walk in the woods near Montignac. As they walked along, one of them noticed an unusual rock. When they got closer, they realized that it wasn't a rock; it was an opening in the ground. This opening led to a cave. The boys decided to have a look around this cave. The walls of the cave were covered with ancient art. The boys didn't know it, but the cave was the find of the century!

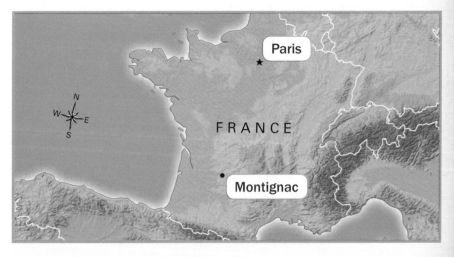

Some cave paintings show large groups of animals.

Over the years, many historians and artists came to study the art. They wanted to understand who painted them and what they might mean. They soon realized that some of the art indicated animals that were on Earth a long time ago. However, these animals no longer exist. Many of the pictures also showed people following animals and trying to kill them for food. In the end, historians agreed this was likely to be the art of a civilization that existed over 15,000 years ago.

By 1950, over a thousand people from all over the world were visiting the caves every day. But by 1955, the paintings were beginning to become difficult to see. Because so many people were passing through the caves, the paintings were losing their color. Sadly, people can no longer visit the caves. However, another set of cave paintings has been created. These paintings look exactly the same as the Lasaux Paintings. People made the paintings so that everyone can still learn about this ancient civilization. If you are near Montignac, these caves and wonderful paintings are a must-see!

CD 2, Track 06

Word Count: 325
Time: _____

Vocabulary List

agents of deterioration (H: 19)

ancestor (H: 10, 19)

ancient (H: 3, 7, 8, 12, 15, 19)

art (H: 3, 4, 7, 10, 12, 15, 16, 19)

artist (H: 3, 7, 10, 16)

bark (H: 16)

civilization (H: 3, 10, 19)

desert (H: 4)

Dreamtime (H: 3, 4, 7, 8, 9, 10, 19)

Earth (H: 3, 7, 12, 15)

famous (H: 16)

fish (H: 15)

guide (H: 12)

hunter (H: 12)

insect (H: 2, 19)

kangaroo (H: 2, 12, 15)

national park (H: 2, 8)

naturalist (H: 10)

rainforest (H: 4)

reptile (H: 2, 19)

rock (H: 2, 4, 7, 8, 9, 10, 16, 19)

season (H: 15)

turtle (H: 2, 15)

The Young Riders
of Mongolia

Rob Waring, *Series Editor*

HEINLE
CENGAGE Learning™

Australia • Brazil • Japan • Korea • Mexico • Singapore • Spain • United Kingdom • United States

Words to Know

This story is set in Mongolia. It happens near Ulan Bator [ulan bɑtɔr], the capital city of Mongolia.

Ulan Bator

MONGOLIA

ASIA

N
W E
S

A **The Parts of a Horse.** Look at the picture. Write the letter of the correct word next to each definition.

1. the part of a horse's body that sticks out from the back: _____

2. the flat part of the face, above the eyes and below the hair: _____

3. the piece of hair that falls forward between a horse's ears: _____

4. the long body parts used for running and walking: _____

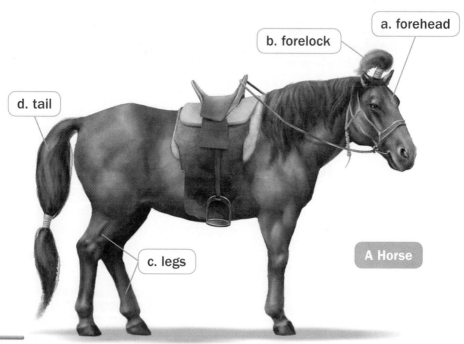

a. forehead

b. forelock

d. tail

c. legs

A Horse

B **An Old Tradition.** Read the paragraph. Then, complete the sentences.

This story is about an interesting horse race in Mongolia. In the race, the riders make their horses run very fast, or gallop. The fastest horse and rider wins the race. The race started in the 1200s, during the times of Genghis Khan. Genghis Khan was the emperor, or king, of a very big empire. Horses were very important in building his empire. He had a large cavalry with many excellent horsemen. Because of this, the sport of horseback riding continues to be very important to many Mongolians today.

1. People from Mongolia are called M_____ .

2. When horses run very fast they g_____ .

3. An event to see who is fastest is a r_____ .

4. An area ruled by one person is an e_____ .

5. The sport of riding horses is called h_____ r_____ .

6. The man who rules an empire is an e_____ .

7. A group of men who fight on horseback is a c_____ .

Genghis Khan
(c. 1162–1227)

A Horse and Rider

Mongolians are very good at horseback riding. People all over the world think that they're great horsemen. It's something that has always been a part of Mongolian culture, even in the 1200s. In the days of the emperor Genghis Khan, Mongolia had a very strong cavalry. This cavalry helped the emperor to create one of the largest empires ever known.

Since the days of Genghis Khan, life on the quiet **steppes**[1] of Mongolia has changed. Horses are still a very important part of the culture here. Many people often move from place to place. They need horses for their way of life, just as they did centuries ago.

---

[1]**steppe:** a large area of land with grass but no trees

 CD 2, Track 07

Long ago, Mongolia had a very strong cavalry.

In Mongolia, the people sometimes have events to show just how important horses are to them. Each year in July, thousands of people come from all over Mongolia to a place just outside the city of Ulan Bator. They come for the **festival**[2] of **Naadam**.[3] This festival has several important events in traditional Mongolian sports—including horseback riding. However, the Naadam race is a little unusual because the 'horsemen' at this event are just children. The riders must be less than 12 years old!

---

[2]**festival:** special day or time with special activities
[3]**Naadam:** [nɑdɑm]

What do you think?

1. Are there any festivals in your country?

2. What events do they have?

3. Are there any special activities especially for young people?

On the day of the race, careful and detailed preparations begin early in the morning. The horses have to look very special. The racers cover each horse's tail with **leather**.[4] They also cover the forelock on the horse's forehead. Then, people offer horse's milk to the spirits of nature. Horse's milk has an important meaning in Mongolian culture. After that, they use **incense**[5] to clean the area around the rider of bad spirits. Finally, they put a drop of this special milk near the legs to protect the rider and horse. At last the horses and riders are ready for the big race.

---

[4]**leather:** animal skin often used to make shoes
[5]**incense:** a substance that is burnt to produce a sweet smell

leather

Before the race, the parents of the young riders join them to walk around a special area. It's an important day and the mothers and fathers want to see the race. Every parent hopes that their child will be one of the winners.

It's a big event—about 500 riders will compete in the first race. It's a demanding event too; before the riders can even begin the race, they must walk the horses over **15 miles**[6] to the starting point.

---

[6] **15 miles:** 24.1 kilometers

Finally, the race begins. People wait at the finish line to watch the race. However, they can't see anything at first. The race is so long that it's actually happening miles away. The horses and riders are galloping towards the finish.

The viewers want to get near the winning horses. An old story says that the **dust**[7] that rises into the air when the horses run is special. People believe that it brings happiness and success to anybody it touches.

---

[7]**dust:** small, dry pieces of earth

After some time, the first horses and riders appear. It's been a very long race. These first riders have already been galloping for nearly 30 minutes!

The first five horses to finish the race will get a blue **sash**[8] for winning. The winners start to arrive, but the race won't finish for a long time. The other 500 or so horses and riders will keep coming in for another hour.

---

[8]**sash:** a long, thin piece of cloth

Identify the Main Ideas

Skim the story. Find three unusual things about the race at the Naadam Festival. Make a list.

The Naadam race finishes at the National Stadium, the country's main sports ground. There is a lovely party with a lot of music. A singer sings about the winning horses and how good they are. The winners walk around the sports ground. They're very pleased. They receive **medals**[9] and horse's milk.

---

[9]**medal:** a special circle of metal given to winners of a race

singer

It's the end of the Naadam race for another year. The race is very demanding for everyone involved. Indeed, these young riders are not just any children. They have shown their **skills**[10] in one of Mongolia's most important traditions. They've shown that they may just be the next great riders of Mongolia!

---

[10]**skill:** ability to do an activity or job well

After You Read

1. On page I4, 'they' in paragraph one refers to:
    A. people all over the world
    B. horsemen
    C. Mongolians
    D. horses

2. Today in Mongolia, _____ has changed since Genghis Khan.
    A. a lot
    B. little
    C. nothing
    D. everything

3. What is unusual about the riders in the festival of Naadam?
    A. They are good horsemen.
    B. They are Mongolians.
    C. They are women.
    D. They are children.

4. When is the festival of Naadam every year?
    A. January
    B. June
    C. July
    D. August

5. Which of the following is NOT part of preparing a horse for the festival?
    A. Incense cleans the area of bad spirits.
    B. The color of the tail is changed.
    C. The forelock is covered in leather.
    D. Horse's milk is offered to spirits.

6. On page I10, 'them' in paragraph one refers to:
    A. the riders
    B. the horses
    C. the parents
    D. the horses and riders

7. On page 113, the word 'begin' in paragraph one means:
  A. start
  B. do
  C. prepare
  D. join

8. People believe that the dust brings happiness to _____ it touches.
  A. nobody
  B. some people
  C. successful people
  D. anybody

9. What is a good heading for page 114?
  A. The First Riders Appear Quickly
  B. Riders Are Tired After the Horse Race
  C. A Very Long Race for the Young Riders
  D. Winners Come After One Hour

10. In the story, how do the young winners feel after the race?
  A. tired
  B. pleased
  C. young
  D. energetic

11. According to the story, what is one of Mongolia's most important traditions?
  A. creating empires
  B. drinking horse milk
  C. singing in the National Stadium
  D. horse racing

Genghis Khan

G enghis Khan was born in about 1165 in what is now called Mongolia. His life was not an easy one. His father was killed when Genghis was only nine years old. He then became responsible for his family. His mother taught him how to protect the family. This education was useful when he governed the empire that he created in later life. Genghis Khan was one of history's strongest leaders. He was responsible for bringing the Mongolian people together into a single nation. He achieved this by the time he was 30 years old.

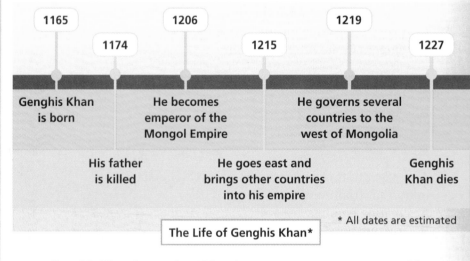

1165	1174	1206	1215	1219	1227
Genghis Khan is born	His father is killed	He becomes emperor of the Mongol Empire	He goes east and brings other countries into his empire	He governs several countries to the west of Mongolia	Genghis Khan dies

* All dates are estimated

The Life of Genghis Khan*

Genghis Khan learned to ride a horse at a very young age and he taught his men how to ride as well. Their horseback riding skills are well-known. His cavalry was one of the strongest and most fearless in the world. With the help of these men, this emperor changed Asia and the Middle East.

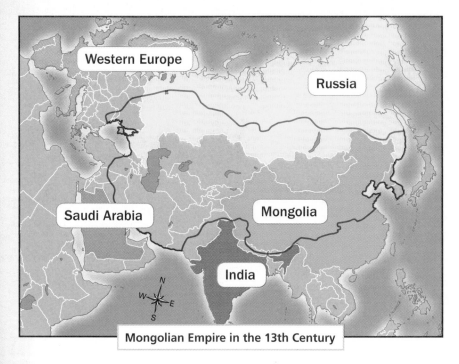

Mongolian Empire in the 13th Century

Genghis Khan created one of the largest empires in history. It started in Korea on the east and went all the way to Western Europe. During the Mongolian Wars, he and his cavalry moved across Asia and the Middle East. Khan then added each new country they entered to his empire. At one point, Khan's empire included parts of the countries we call China, Korea, Russia, and Mongolia.

Genghis Khan also achieved many other things. He set up the first trade agreements among the countries of Asia and the Middle East. He supported arts like painting. He even established a handwriting system for the Mongolian language. Over time, this led to increased trade and learning. To some people Genghis Khan was only a strong fighter, to others he was a lot more.

CD 2, Track 08

Word Count: 322
Time: _____

Vocabulary List

dust (l: 13)

emperor (l: 3, 4)

empire (l: 3, 4)

festival (l: 6, 15)

forehead (l: 2, 9)

forelock (l: 2, 9)

gallop (l: 3, 14)

horseback riding (l: 3, 4)

incense (l: 9)

leather (l: 9)

leg (l: 2, 9)

medal (l: 17)

Mongolian (l: 3, 4, 6, 9)

race (l: 3, 6, 9, 10, 13, 14, 17, 18)

sash (l: 15)

skill (l: 18)

steppe (l: 4)

tail (l: 2, 9)

Alaskan
ICE CLIMBING

Rob Waring, *Series Editor*

HEINLE
CENGAGE Learning

Australia • Brazil • Japan • Korea • Mexico • Singapore • Spain • United Kingdom • United States

Words to Know

This story starts in Talkeetna [tælkitnə] Alaska, in the United States (U.S.). It ends in an area called Matanuska [mætənuskə], near Denali [dənɑli] National Park.

A **In the Mountains.** Here are some activities you can do on a mountain or a glacier. Match the words in the box to the correct picture.

| climbing | hiking | skiing |

1. _____

2. _____

3. _____

The Matanuska **Glacier** is over 27 miles long.

B **Mountain Weather Conditions.** **Weather** refers to the conditions of the sky and air. Match each weather word to the correct definition.

1. cloud: _____	**a.** the light from the sun
2. fine: _____	**b.** very cold water that has become hard
3. fog: _____	**c.** a natural, fast movement of air
4. ice: _____	**d.** white frozen water that falls from the sky in cold weather
5. rain: _____	**e.** a white or gray mass in the air made of small drops of water
6. snow: _____	**f.** drops of water falling from the sky
7. sunshine: _____	**g.** good or nice
8. wind: _____	**h.** a heavy gray mass near the ground that makes it difficult to see

The tallest **mountain** in North America is over 20,000 feet tall.

Mount McKinley

1 mile = 1,609 meters
1 foot = 0.30 meters

There's only one thing that's certain about the weather in Alaska—it changes all the time! Sometimes there's rain, sometimes there's wind, sometimes there's snow. Sometimes the weather is just fine with lots of sunshine.

On one particular day, there's rain and fog all the way from Denali National Park to the town of Talkeetna. There, a group of visitors is planning to fly onto a glacier. They then want to ski down the glacier. But the weather has other plans …

CD 2, Track 09

The group really wants to get to the glacier to ski. "So, can we go today?" one of them asks. But the answer is not a good one. "Uh, not until the **pilots**[1] are comfortable with the weather," replies their **guide**[2] Colby Coombs. He then explains that the clouds are too low, so the group cannot fly. It's too unsafe.

Colby Coombs and Caitlin Palmer are both experienced mountain guides. They run a climbing school. They teach beginner climbers and help experienced climbers to reach the top of Denali. Denali is a mountain that is also known as Mount McKinley. It's the highest mountain in North America.

---

[1]**pilot:** a person who operates an airplane
[2]**guide:** a person whose job is showing places to visitors

Colby and Caitlin are both very good climbers. They're not usually doubtful when they're in the mountains. But even they won't take a small plane out in bad weather. "It's kind of **ornery**[3] weather," says, Colby. "You usually have to **factor in**[4] a day or two to **put up with**[5] bad weather."

So, Colby and Caitlin decide on another plan. Instead of taking the group to ski down a glacier, they will take them to climb up one. They plan to take the group to a glacier that they can drive to by car: the Matanuska glacier.

---

[3] **ornery:** bad
[4] **factor in:** include
[5] **put up with:** take into consideration; allow for

Infer Meaning

Read the second paragraph on page J8 again. Analyze the phrase below. To what does each underlined word refer?

"they will take them to climb up one"

Matanuska is a very big glacier—it's 27 miles long and two miles wide. The name 'Matanuska' comes from an old Russian word for the **Athabascan Indians**[6] who live in the area. The glacier is in a low area that has many trees around it. It formed 2,000 years ago, but it's always moving and changing. It's also always difficult to climb.

---

[6]**Athabascan Indians:** [æθəbæskən ɪndiənz] a group of native people who live in Alaska

The group gets ready to climb one of the Matanuska glacier's formations—a 30-foot wall of ice. At the base of the wall, Caitlin explains how to climb it, and it's not going to be easy. "The most **stable**[7] you're going to be is when you have all the points of your **crampons**[8] sticking on the ice," says Caitlin.

Caitlin then suggests ways to use crampons. They can help people climb up ice securely and safely. "Front points in … **heels**[9] down," she says. "And if you're going to place a tool," she adds, "[place it] really solid[ly]."

---

[7]**stable:** strong; secure
[8]**crampon:** a kind of climbing tool for ice or snow that fits on the shoe
[9]**heel:** the rounded back part of the foot

tool

wall of ice

heels

front points

crampon

The hike across Matanuska is beautiful, but it can also be very unsafe. One summer, a young man fell into an opening in the ice called a **cirque**,[10] and died.

There are also stories of beginner hikers who get lost and almost die from the cold. In addition, there are **crevasses**[11] everywhere. The climbers have to be careful; they could easily fall in. If they fall into a crevasse, it will be very difficult to get out. Perhaps it will be impossible.

---

[10] **cirque:** [sɜrk] a round opening in the ice
[11] **crevasse:** a long deep opening in the thick ice of a glacier

The group walks slowly and carefully across the glacier. It's very cold; they have to keep moving to stay warm. Finally, they reach solid ice. They're finally at **the heart of**[12] the glacier.

At this point, the climbers have a wonderful view. They can see a glacial lake with many **seracs**[13] in the background. Seracs are large pieces of blue glacial ice that stick up in the air. The glacier creates these seracs as it slowly moves.

Colby explains that an area with many seracs is called an 'ice fall.' He also adds that the seracs can make the area unsafe. This is because they are very big and may fall. He says that a good climber would not hike below an ice fall. It's just not safe.

---

[12]**the heart of:** the center of
[13]**serac:** [sɪræk] a large piece of glacial ice

crevasse

The group enjoys climbing the glacier. It's hard work, but Colby and Caitlin make it look easy. It's a very special feeling when the members of the group reach the top of another ice wall. "OK, I made it!" says one of the beginner climbers happily.

Alaska is home to a large number of glaciers, about 100,000 in total. The people in this group can now say that they have successfully climbed one of them—Matanuska. Now, they only have 99,999 more glaciers to climb!

What do you think?

1. Would you like to climb a glacier?

2. Why or why not?

3. Imagine you are going to climb a glacier. What three things will you bring?

After You Read

1. What kind of weather is usual in Alaska?
   A. rain
   B. snow
   C. fog
   D. all of the above

2. On page J4, the word 'it' refers to:
   A. a plane
   B. a glacier
   C. the weather
   D. Denali National Park

3. What is another name for Denali?
   A. Mount McKinley
   B. Athabascan
   C. Alaska
   D. North America

4. Why does the group decide to drive to another glacier?
   A. They don't like to fly on planes.
   B. The Matanuska glacier is too far away.
   C. They are going to ski down the glacier.
   D. The weather is too unsafe to fly.

5. What is a good heading for page J11?
   A. The High Area Glacier
   B. Skiing and Climbing Guides
   C. About Matanuska
   D. 2,000 Year Old Tree

6. Which is NOT true about Matanuska?
   A. The glacier's name comes from an old Russian word.
   B. There are only a few trees in the glacier's low area.
   C. The glacier is 2 miles wide and 27 miles long.
   D. The glacier is always changing.

7. On page J12, what does the word 'explains' mean?
   A. decides
   B. guesses
   C. thinks
   D. teaches

8. Which of the following is NOT dangerous on the glacier?
   A. crevasse
   B. cirque
   C. crampon
   D. ice fall

9. What does Colby think about an area with many seracs?
   A. A good climber will not hike there.
   B. A new climber can hike there easily.
   C. A good climber will stop and rest there.
   D. A good climber likes to climb ice falls.

10. The phrase 'very special' on page J18 can be replaced by:
    A. cold
    B. wonderful
    C. common
    D. unsafe

11. In this story, people _____ across and _____ up a glacier.
    A. drive, fly
    B. fly, ski
    C. hike, climb
    D. ski, climb

Ice Climbing for
BEGINNERS

Ice climbing is similar to mountain climbing. However, instead of being on hard stone, ice climbers move up, down, and even across walls of cold, glassy ice. There are two types of ice climbing. The first type involves climbing over ice and hard snow on the side of a mountain or glacier. The second type involves climbing up water that has become ice—for example a frozen waterfall. Climbers say that both can be difficult and that both require very serious attention.

A Frozen Waterfall

ice ax

boots

rope

Ice climbers need good boots, strong ropes, and an ice ax.

One difficult thing about ice climbing is that the ice in one place can change from day to day. It can, even change from hour to hour. The best way to go up a wall of ice in the morning may not be the best way to come down again later. Ice climbers have to learn how to see differences in the ice. They also must be able to change their plans accordingly.

Three things are very important to help keep ice climbers safe when they climb. First of all, they need special boots to keep their feet warm. These boots also help stop them from falling when they put their feet down on the ice. Secondly, ice climbers need an ice ax. They can use the ax to make small openings in the ice. They can then carefully place

their feet in the openings. The third important thing they need is a rope system. Climbers often only use one rope, but sometimes they use two.

Now let's take a look at something special that all ice climbers put on their boots—crampons. Crampons hold climbers' feet securely as they place them on the ice. The crampons actually go into the ice and give the climber a secure place to step. People say that crampons are responsible for saving many climbers' lives because they stop them from falling.

CD 2, Track 10

Word Count: 309
Time: _____

Vocabulary List

cirque (J: 15)
climb (J: 2, 7, 8, 9, 11, 15, 16, 18)
crampon (J: 12)
crevase (J: 15)
factor in (J: 8)
fine (J: 3, 4)
fog (J: 3, 4)
glacier (J: 2, 4, 7, 8, 11, 12, 15, 16, 18)
heel (J: 12)
hike (J: 2, 15, 16)
ice (J: 3, 12, 13, 15, 16)
mile (J: 3, 11)
national park (J: 2, 4)
ornery (J: 8)
pilot (J: 7)
put up with (J: 8)
rain (J: 3, 4)
serac (J: 16, 18)
ski (J: 2, 4, 8)
snow (J: 3, 4, 12)
stable (J: 12)
sunshine (J: 3, 4)
the heart of (J: 16)
wind (J: 3, 4)

Don't Believe
YOUR EYES!

Rob Waring, *Series Editor*

HEINLE
CENGAGE Learning

Australia • Brazil • Japan • Korea • Mexico • Singapore • Spain • United Kingdom • United States

Words to Know

This story is set in Italy, near Genoa [dʒɛnoʊə]. It happens in the small town of Camogli [kɑmɔlyi] in the Liguria [lɪgyuɔriə] area.

Mediterranean Sea

A **Is it real?** Complete the paragraph with the words in the box.

art	coast	technique
artists	fishermen	village

    Camogli is a small town, or (1)_____, in northern Italy. Camogli is on the (2)_____. It's next to the Mediterranean Sea. Many people who live in the town are (3)_____. Their job is catching fish and seafood. However, there are also several (4)_____ in the town. They create beautiful paintings and other pieces of (5)_____. They're famous for a special realistic way of painting. The (6)_____ is called *trompe l'oeil* [trɔmp lɔɪ]. Viewers often think these paintings are real things, but they're not. Look at the pictures. Which one is the photo? Which one is *trompe l'oeil*?

A Painting and a Photograph

B **Italian Homes.** Read the definitions. Label the items in the picture with the underlined words.

A <u>balcony</u> is a small area outside a higher-level room that one can stand or sit on.
A <u>façade</u> is the front of a large building.
A <u>terrace</u> is a flat area outside a house where you can sit.
A <u>wall</u> is one of the sides of a room or building.
A <u>window</u> is a space that has glass in it to let light and air inside.

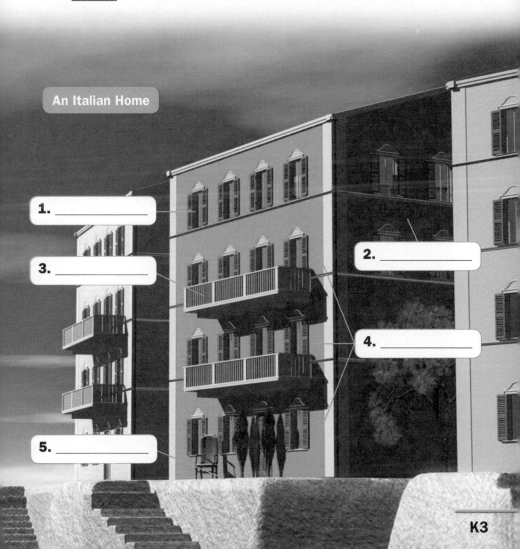

An Italian Home

1. _____

2. _____

3. _____

4. _____

5. _____

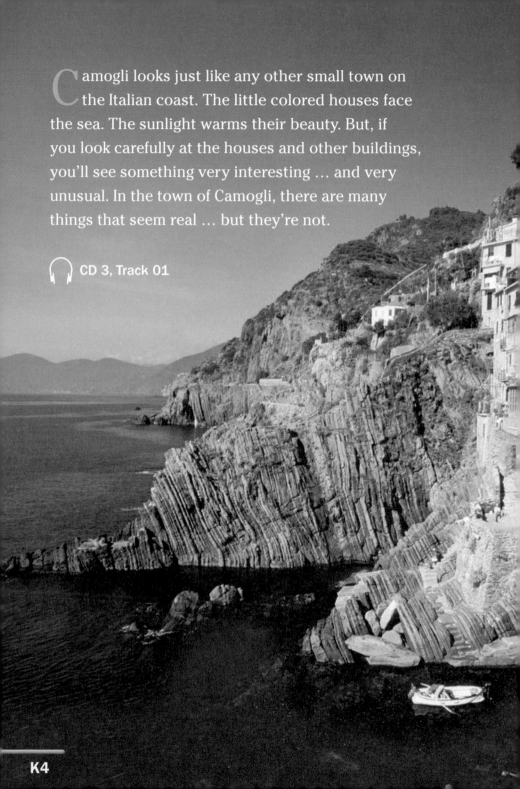

Camogli looks just like any other small town on the Italian coast. The little colored houses face the sea. The sunlight warms their beauty. But, if you look carefully at the houses and other buildings, you'll see something very interesting … and very unusual. In the town of Camogli, there are many things that seem real … but they're not.

CD 3, Track 01

K4

K5

This fishing village near Genoa is full of *trompe l'oeil*—a type of art in which nothing is what it seems to be. For example, windows open—in **solid**[1] walls. There seems to be **elaborate**[2] stonework—but it isn't stonework—it's paint! And while some flowers die, other flowers live for years. Why? Because they're painted on the building!

[1] **solid:** hard and firm; without holes or spaces
[2] **elaborate:** detailed; made carefully from many parts

Predict

Answer the question. Then, scan page K9 to check your answers.

What are two reasons that people painted their houses with *trompe l'oeil* in the past?

Trompe l'oeil has been around for a long time. In the past, Camogli's fishermen used to paint their houses in **bright**[3] colors and unusual designs. They included things like elaborate façades and balconies on them as well. They did this so that they could see their homes easily from the water. Then, in the 1700s, this style of art became a way to make small, simple buildings look **grand**.[4] It also made them seem like they cost a lot of money.

But what about today? Well, there are still thousands of *trompe l'oeil* houses in this area of Italy. However now, there are only a few artists that are available to paint them. **Raffaella Stracca**[5] is one of these artists.

---

[3] **bright:** having a strong, light color
[4] **grand:** very large and special
[5] **Raffaella Stracca:** [rɑfaɪɛlə strɑkə]

Trompe l'oeil is in Raffaella's family. She learned this special technique, or style of painting, from her grandmother. Raffaella has not forgotten the history of *trompe l'oeil* either. She uses a mixture of old and new methods to create her work.

Raffaella says that *trompe l'oeil* is a tradition that has started to return. "You find a lot of these painted façades in the area of Liguria—a lot!" she explains. "But for a while, it seemed like no one was doing them anymore," she adds.

Becoming a good *trompe l'oeil* painter is difficult. It takes a lot of time and a lot of study. Raffaella has worked for 20 years to be able to paint stone so well that it looks real—even when you stand close to it. Like most painters, Raffaella learned *trompe l'oeil* from other artists, not in a school. However, this has become an issue these days. There are now fewer artists. Therefore, there are fewer teachers, and fewer places for new painters to learn.

It takes a lot of time to be able to paint stone that seems real.

K11

In the city of Florence, the **Palazzo Spinelli**[6] Art School has one of the few *trompe l'oeil* programs available. There, painters study for a full year to learn how to create everything from *trompe l'oeil* stonework to **fake**[7] doors.

Most students at this school are international; they have come from other countries to learn the technique. However, they do understand that the technique is a very 'Italian' tradition. One visiting student explains, "I haven't seen anywhere else in the world [with] as much *trompe l'oeil* and **mural**[8] painting as [I've seen] here in Italy."

[6]**Palazzo Spinelli:** [pəlɑtsoʊ spinɛli]
[7]**fake:** not real
[8]**mural:** a painting that covers the wall of a building

K13

K14

Carlo Pere[9] is one artist who studied *trompe l'oeil* and now he's made a business out of it. His customers are often people who live in small houses or city apartments. They want to buy Pere's *trompe l'oeil* terraces and balconies to improve the appearance of their homes. Pere's *trompe l'oeil* projects can make a small apartment look much bigger.

But it's not just about appearance. Carlo feels that the purpose of *trompe l'oeil* is to bring something unexpected to a new place. He explains his feelings. "*Trompe l'oeil* means bringing the central city of Milan to the sea," he says, "or the sea to the **mountains**[10] ... or even the mountains to the sea."

---

[9]**Carlo Pere:** [kɑrloʊ pɛreɪ]
[10]**mountain:** a very high hill

K16

Carlo's painting style comes from history and the past. He uses an art book from the 1300s to study the theory of the technique. He only uses traditional-style paints and mixes them by hand.

He does all of this for one reason: to protect the *trompe l'oeil* traditions. He also believes that art should be for everyone. "It's easy to see," he says. "If we lose the *trompe l'oeil* tradition, then very little of Camogli's culture will remain. We'll have **museums**,[11] but that's not much." According to Carlo, "Culture should be seen, everyone should enjoy it."

---

[11] **museum:** a building where people can look at things related to art, history, or science

Fact Check:

1. What kind of homes do Carlo Pere's customers have?

2. What kinds of things does he paint?

3. How does Pere define *trompe l'oeil*?

4. Why does Carlo use traditional-style paints?

K18

Fortunately, in this part of Italy, you can still see the local art and culture everywhere. It's in the streets, in the **bay**,[12] and in the **cafés**.[13] But remember, in Camogli, what you see may not be what you think it is—so don't always believe your eyes!

[12] **bay:** an area of coast where the land curves in
[13] **café:** a restaurant that serves simple food and drinks

After You Read

1. On page K4, 'they're' refers to:
   A. the things in Camogli
   B. the people of Camogli
   C. the houses in Camogli
   D. the things in the sea

2. The purpose of the descriptions on page K6 is to:
   A. explain *trompe l'oeil* in detail
   B. show that some flowers can die
   C. give an example of Italian stonework
   D. show that *trompe l'oeil* is solid

3. Which is NOT a reason why *trompe l'oeil* began?
   A. Fishermen wanted to see their homes from the sea.
   B. People wanted their houses to look expensive.
   C. Designs and bright colors made homes look grand.
   D. In the 1700s, fishermen only liked bright colors.

4. In the area of Liguria, there are _____ painted façades.
   A. some
   B. many
   C. a few
   D. no

5. A good heading for page K10 is:
   A. Raffaella Learned the Techniques Quickly
   B. Fewer Teachers Equals Fewer Artists
   C. Raffaella Teaches Façade Painting
   D. Many Places to Learn Italian Art

6. Most art students believe that mural painting is:
   A. traditionally Italian
   B. not from Italy
   C. for Italians only
   D. easy to learn

7. A type of place that Carlo Pere often improves is:
 A. a big office building
 B. a house with a large terrace
 C. a home with lots of art
 D. an apartment with no balcony

8. Who are 'they' in paragraph one on page K15?
 A. artists
 B. people with terraces
 C. customers
 D. businesses

9. On page K17, the word 'reason' in paragraph two means:
 A. technique
 B. purpose
 C. situation
 D. tradition

10. What does Carlo Pere believe about culture?
 A. Everyone should see and enjoy it.
 B. Museums are the best place for it
 C. It is hard to teach everyone.
 D. Books are the best place to see it.

11. The writer probably thinks that Camogli is a:
 A. beautiful village on the coast
 B. special fishing town
 C. town with too many artists
 D. place without culture

MY NEW ART SCHOOL

Hi Everyone!

I can't believe that I'm actually here in France learning how to paint! It's really beautiful here. I've always loved art, but this is the first time I've ever taken painting lessons. There are six students in my class. We're staying in the home of a French couple in the Jura Mountains. Mr. and Mrs. Gautier are artists and they teach an art class just for us every morning. I'm learning some wonderful painting techniques. Later in the day, we visit local villages in the area. We get to spend hours enjoying the views while we paint what we see. Yesterday, I painted a beautiful village picture. I think it's quite nice!

The Jura Mountains

Painting Class

Oh, and the house we are staying in is so lovely! Mrs. Gautier's family built it in the eighteenth century. I've never seen anything like it. It looks like something in a film! It's very large and the façade has a lot of elaborate stonework. Instead of windows, all the rooms have glass doors. The best part is that each set of doors opens onto a balcony. It's just wonderful! You know me. I always sleep for a long time in the morning. But here, I get up early and sit on my balcony, just so I can watch the sun rise.

We spend a lot of our time on the private terrace in front of the house. It has become my favorite place because it's so quiet. We often eat out there and it's where we have our painting classes. Sometimes we just sit on the terrace in the evening talking and enjoying the moment. I've never had an experience quite like this, but I plan to come back again. Maybe you can join me next time. I've included a couple of pictures that I took. I hope you enjoy them.

See you soon!
Carol

CD 3, Track 02

Word Count: 308
Time: _____

Vocabulary List

art (K: 2, 6, 9, 12, 17, 19)
artist (K: 2, 9, 10, 15)
balcony (K: 3, 9, 15)
bay (K: 19)
bright (K: 9)
café (K: 19)
coast (K: 2, 4)
elaborate (K: 6, 9)
façade (K: 3, 9, 10)
fake (K: 12)
fishermen (K: 2, 9)
grand (K: 9)
mountain (K: 15)
mural (K: 12)
museum (K: 17)
solid (K: 6)
technique (K: 2, 10, 12, 17)
terrace (K: 3, 15)
village (K: 2, 6)
wall (K: 3, 6)
window (K: 3, 6)

The Story of
THE HULA

Rob Waring, *Series Editor*

HEINLE
CENGAGE Learning™

Australia • Brazil • Japan • Korea • Mexico • Singapore • Spain • United Kingdom • United States

L1

Words to Know

This story is set in the United States (U.S.), in the state of Hawaii [həwɑi]. In the story, you will also read about the city of Hilo [hilou].

HAWAII

PACIFIC OCEAN

Hilo

NORTH AMERICA

Hawaii

SOUTH AMERICA

N
W—E
S

 The Hawaiian Islands. Read the paragraph. Then, match each word with the correct definition.

Hawaii is a group of islands in the Pacific Ocean. The islands are in a tropical area, which means that it is very hot there. Hawaii has water all around it, so it has many beautiful beaches. It is also a land with an ancient history and culture. Long ago, Hawaii had kings and queens that ruled the island. They were very powerful leaders. There are many legends in Hawaii as well. They tell interesting stories about the past.

1. island _____

2. ocean _____

3. tropical _____

4. beach _____

5. ancient _____

6. queen _____

7. legend _____

a. a woman ruler

b. very old

c. a very large body of water; a sea

d. an old story from the past

e. an area of sand or stones next to the sea

f. from or in the hottest parts of the world

g. an area of land that has water around it

B **Hula Dancers.** Read the sentences. Then complete the paragraph with the underlined words.

The hula (hulə) is a kind of dance.
A *halau* (hə'lau) is a school where they teach the hula.
Hula dancers wear special costumes.
Hawaiian people dance the hula at special events called festivals.
Spiritual means with strong feelings or beliefs.

In Hawaii, the hula is a very important traditional (1) _____. It's more than three hundred years old. Nowadays, Hawaiians dance the hula at (2) _____. For some, the hula is a (3) _____ dance that they relate to personal beliefs and feelings. People can learn the hula at a (4) _____. Most hula dancers wear beautiful (5) _____ and put flowers in their hair.

A Tropical Island

Hawaiian Hula Dancers

Hawaii is a truly beautiful place. Most people know Hawaii for its lovely beaches and its warm ocean. However, Hawaii is also a land full of legends. Several old stories have existed for many years on these tropical islands. One of the oldest legends tells of a special dance called the hula, which started here more than three hundred years ago.

🎧 CD 3, Track 03

One hula teacher tells the story of how the dance started. "The hula started, as far as legend tells it, when **Hi'iaki**[1] and her good friend **Hopoe**[2] went down to the beach. And then, when they were there, they noticed the waves … and they **imitated**[3] the waves. And then they started to use their hands … like **portraying**[4] the waves. That's how the hula started."

_____

[1]**Hi'iaki:** [hɪʔiɑki]
[2]**Hopoe:** [houpouaɪ]
[3]**imitate:** behave in a similar way as someone or something else
[4]**portray:** show; act like

ocean

waves

beach

Sequence the Events

What is the correct order of the events? Read page L9, then number 1 to 4.

_____ The queen banned the hula.

_____ The religious people were surprised.

_____ Dancers performed the hula in secret.

_____ Religious people came to Hawaii.

However, not everyone has always liked the hula. In 1820, very **religious**[5] people from Western countries came to Hawaii. They were surprised by the hula because the dancers were not wearing many clothes. The visitors were so surprised, that they asked the queen of Hawaii to **ban**[6] the dance.

After that, most Hawaiians were not allowed to perform the hula in public for almost sixty years. But that did not mean the dancing stopped. Many dancers still performed the hula **in secret**.[7] The dance was always there.

---

[5] **religious:** believing in God or gods
[6] **ban:** not allow; stop
[7] **in secret:** not seen or known about by most people

Years later, things have changed. At the moment, there is a renewed interest in Hawaiian culture throughout these islands. People of all ages want to study the ancient culture. They want to learn how to dance the hula.

This interest has resulted in an increase in the demand for hula lessons. So, more and more people are attending *halaus*. *Halaus* are special schools that teach the hula in the traditional way. These schools also teach the traditional values, and **discipline**,[8] that go along with the dance.

---

[8]**discipline:** rules and control

The hula isn't an easy dance to do. First, the dancers must work very hard to learn it. Then, they have to practice for many hours. If they want to perform the dance for other people, they must be ready.

One person who can help dancers prepare is **Kumano Palani Kulala**.[9] Kumano is a hula teacher. For him, the dance is a way to bring the best of ancient Hawaiian culture to people today.

---

[9]**Kumano Palani Kulala:** [kumɑnoʊ pəlɑni kulɑlə]

Kumano says that the dance is not really about the body. He feels that it's more about the mind. He also feels that it's a very spiritual dance. He explains his feelings: " ... the hula is more ... not so much a **physical** [10] thing, but more of a **mental** [11] and a spiritual thing. For [new dancers], the dancing means very little, because for Hawaiians today, many of them don't speak the [Hawaiian] language. So, what I try to do is to bring to mind the reality that they see today."

[10] **physical:** of the body
[11] **mental:** of the mind

Fact Check: True or false?

1. Dancers have to practice a lot.

2. Kumano Palini Kulala is a hula teacher.

3. The hula is only a physical thing.

4. Many Hawaiians don't speak the Hawaiian language.

With the help of people like Kumano, the hula has become an important part of Hawaiian life and culture once again. Because of this, there are now many hula festivals in Hawaii. Every year, the most important hula **competition**[12] happens in the city of Hilo. Dancers from all of the Hawaiian Islands come together at this festival. The festival is held in the name of a legendary Hawaiian king. This king helped to return the ancient hula to its place at the center of Hawaiian culture.

In the competition, of course the **judges**[13] look at the way the dancers dance. But they look at more than that. They also look at the dancers' costumes and their style. The way the person wears a skirt, the color of his or her costume, and the flowers they wear are all very important.

---

[12] **competition:** an event in which people try to be the best and win
[13] **judge:** someone who decides which person or thing wins

flowers

skirt

judges

L17

Today in Hawaii, the ancient hula dance is definitely not done in secret; it's a part of everyday life. It's once again a tradition that people can practice and perform often. It's a tradition that they can see at various festivals. And hopefully, it's a tradition that will continue for years and years to come.

After You Read

1. The hula was created in Hawaii _____ three hundred years ago.
   A. more than
   B. exactly
   C. under
   D. less than

2. Which is NOT a good heading for page L6?
   A. Teacher Doesn't Like Ancient Hula Story
   B. Legend of Hula Dance Began on the Beach
   C. Two Girls See Waves and Make a New Dance
   D. Hi'iaki and Hopoe Imitate the Beach

3. What happened to the hula dancers after the queen banned the dance?
   A. They stopped dancing.
   B. They danced in secret.
   C. They started wearing more clothes.
   D. They performed for everyone.

4. The visitors that came from Western countries in 1820 probably came from:
   A. Hawaii
   B. Asia
   C. Europe or the United States
   D. Africa

5. In paragraph 1 on page L9, 'they' refers to:
   A. hula dancers
   B. the queens
   C. Hawaiians
   D. the visitors

6. The writer thinks that learning to dance the hula is:
   A. difficult work
   B. easy work
   C. secretive work
   D. traditional work

7. What does Kumano believe are the most important parts of dancing the hula?
- **A.** the mind and the spirit
- **B.** the body and the spirit
- **C.** the mind and the body
- **D.** the language and the spirit

8. What happens in Hilo every year?
- **A.** a big dancing event
- **B.** a competition
- **C.** a festival for a king
- **D.** all of the above

9. In paragraph 1 on page L16, 'return' means:
- **A.** bring back
- **B.** continue
- **C.** go home
- **D.** celebrate

10. In the competition, the judges look at more than_____ a person dances.
- **A.** when
- **B.** how
- **C.** why
- **D.** where

11. What is the purpose of this story?
- **A.** to show that tradition is important
- **B.** to celebrate a great king
- **C.** to teach an ancient legend
- **D.** to show that competitions are good

TRAVEL News
CARNIVAL IN TRINIDAD

Carnival in Trinidad is one of the longest and happiest parties you could possibly attend. It starts in December and goes on until February. Every year people from all over the world come to this festival. They come to enjoy the great music and unusual food. If you decide to visit Trinidad, you may also have the chance to join the party on this beautiful tropical island.

Kings and Queens Costume Competition

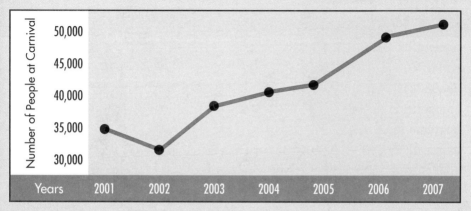

Rising Attendance at Carnival in Trinidad

The main events happen at the end of Carnival. One of the most interesting events is the 'Kings and Queens Costume Competition.' All of the musical groups from the Carnival have their own king and queen. This couple then appears in costume with their musical group. The costumes cost hundreds of U.S. dollars and take many months to create. Some of them are over thirty feet high! Every year, judges choose the best costumes.

In the beginning, Carnival had a religious purpose and the local churches organized the events. However, the people of Trinidad and Tobago originally came from many different cultures. Because of this, they soon began to incorporate other traditions. These traditions came from different parts of the world including South America, Africa, England, France, and India.

This makes Carnival one of the most colorful and varied festivals in the world. It also explains why people from so many different countries choose to attend Carnival.

The latest data shows that attendance at Carnival has risen almost every year since 2001. The figures show an increase from around 35,000 people in 2001 to over 50,000 in 2007. Six out of ten visitors to the country come from the United States, Canada, or the United Kingdom. Carnival attracts many people between December and February, but the island's beautiful beaches and ocean bring thousands more visitors all year round.

CD 3 Track 04

Word Count: 317
Time: _____

Vocabulary List

ancient (L: 2, 10, 13, 16, 18)

ban (L: 8, 9)

beach (L: 2, 4, 6)

competition (L: 16)

costume (L: 3, 16)

dance (L: 3, 4, 6, 8, 9, 10, 13, 14, 15, 16, 18)

discipline (L: 10)

festival (L: 3, 16, 18)

halau (L: 3, 10)

imitate (L: 6)

in secret (L: 8, 9, 18)

island (L: 2, 4, 10, 16)

judge (L: 16, 17)

legend (L: 2, 4, 6, 16)

mental (L: 14)

ocean (L: 2, 4)

physical (L: 14, 15)

portray (L: 6)

queen (L: 2, 8, 9)

religious (L: 8, 9)

spiritual (L: 3, 14)

tropical (L: 2, 4)

The Giant's Causeway

Rob Waring, *Series Editor*

Australia • Brazil • Japan • Korea • Mexico • Singapore • Spain • United Kingdom • United States

Words to Know

This story is set in Northern Ireland. It happens in a place called the 'Giant's Causeway.'

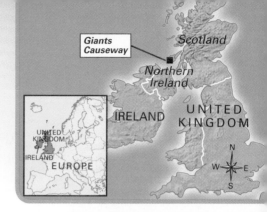

A **Did a Giant Make the Giant's Causeway?** Read the paragraph. Then, complete the sentences with the words in the box.

The Giant's Causeway is a formation made of rock on the Irish coast. There are many legends about who, or what, made it. One story is about a giant called Finn MacCool. According to the story, Finn had a fight with a giant from Scotland. The legend says that Finn MacCool took 40,000 pieces of rock and built a walkway between Northern Ireland and Scotland. People say he did it because he wanted to go to Scotland to find the Scottish giant.

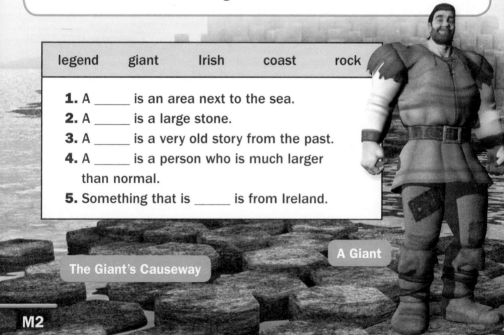

legend	giant	Irish	coast	rock

1. A _____ is an area next to the sea.
2. A _____ is a large stone.
3. A _____ is a very old story from the past.
4. A _____ is a person who is much larger than normal.
5. Something that is _____ is from Ireland.

A Giant

The Giant's Causeway

B Did a Volcano Make the Giant's Causeway? Read the
paragraph. Then match each word with the correct definition.

Scientists are people who study the structure and actions of natural things. Scientists, such as geologists, believe that the Giant's Causeway has a more scientific explanation. One idea is that a volcanic eruption made it. When a volcano erupts, it produces lava. The lava becomes dry and hard and can make interesting formations in the rock. Geologists think the Giant's Causeway is a natural rock formation from a volcano.

1. geologists _____
2. volcano _____
3. erupt _____
4. lava _____
5. formation _____

a. explode; blow up
b. scientists that study the earth
c. hot, melted rock
d. a mountain with a hole in the top
e. things that are arranged in a particular way

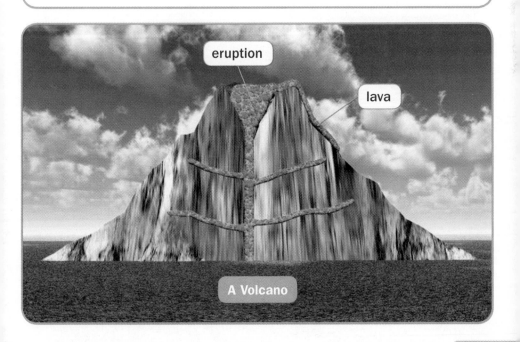

A Volcano

The stone walkway on the coast of Northern Ireland is one of the country's most important **tourist**[1] centers. It's a special place of science and legends. Many visitors come to the area each year. They want to see the Giant's Causeway, Northern Ireland's first **World Heritage Site**.[2]

---

[1] **tourist:** a visitor who travels for enjoyment
[2] **World Heritage Site:** an important cultural place, chosen by the United Nations Educational, Scientific, and Cultural Organization (UNESCO)

🎧 CD 3, Track 05

M5

But where does the Giant's Causeway come from? Why does it exist? People can't agree. There's a big discussion about the beginnings of the walkway. There are people who believe that there is a scientific explanation for it, and there are those who believe in a legend.

For some people, these 40,000 pieces of **basalt**[3] are a natural formation of rock. However, for other people, the Giant's Causeway is the home of an Irish giant named Finn MacCool. But who was he? And why do people say he built the causeway?

---

[3]**basalt:** a kind of rock

M7

In the past, Hill Dick was a **tour guide**[4] for visitors to this beautiful coast. Dick tells the old legend of Finn MacCool. "Finn was one of the great characters in Irish **mythology**[5] or, if you like, Irish fact," says Dick with a smile. He then tells a story about how Finn was angry with a Scottish giant who lived **25 miles**[6] across the sea. So Finn decided to go to Scotland. Finn was not a good swimmer, so he used rocks from volcanoes to build a road to Scotland. He called it the Giant's Causeway.

---

[4]**tour guide:** a person who shows visitors around and gives them information about a place
[5]**mythology:** stories of people from the past
[6]**25 miles:** 40.2 kilometers

Summarize

Close your book. Retell the story of Finn MacCool. Tell it to a partner or write it in a notebook. Use your own words.

Is the legend of Finn MacCool and his causeway true? Did he really build it so that he could catch the Scottish giant? Well, perhaps—if you use your imagination.

However, not everyone agrees with the legend. Scientists like geologist Patrick McKeever have their own, more scientific, story. They say that a volcano made the Giant's Causeway about 60 million years ago. That was a very long time before humans ever lived in this lovely part of the world.

Some people think a volcano erupted and made the Giant's Causeway.

eruption

What do you think?

1. How does McKeever explain the Giant's Causeway?

2. Does he believe the story of Finn MacCool?

3. What makes you think that way?

McKeever tells about what he thinks made the Giant's Causeway. "The lava that was erupted, was erupted very, very quickly and the flows were very, very thick," he says. He then explains that the lava was a bit like **mud**[7] on a hot day. Mud becomes dry and shrinks, or gets smaller when it dries. McKeever says that a similar condition with the lava made the many-sided **columns**.[8] For McKeever and other geologists, the causeway is a natural rock formation.

---

[7]**mud:** a soft combination of water and earth
[8]**column:** a tall post which is made of stone

lava flow

columns

It was much warmer and there was volcanic activity in Northern Ireland 55 to 65 million years ago.

So was it Finn MacCool or a volcano that made the Giant's Causeway? Maybe it doesn't really matter. Tourists from all over the world have been visiting here, and the nearby Irish coast, since the 1800s. These people don't have to believe in the legend—or the scientific explanation—to want to come to this interesting place.

M15

Hill Dick explains why the area has so many visitors. He claims that every visitor has a personal experience when they look at the rocks and the formations they make. He feels that every visitor can make their own personal story about the place. Each visitor has their own experience at the Giant's Causeway because each visitor can use his or her own imagination. "You can **weave**[9] your own story around it," he says. "You can look at a rock and say, 'That, **reminds**[10] me of something … '[or] 'That looks like something … "

---

[9]**weave:** create or make
[10]**remind:** make a person think of something or somebody

Year after year, large numbers of tourists and children visit the Giant's Causeway and listen to the legend of Finn MacCool. As they hear these stories, they begin to wonder about the Giant's Causeway … and where it really came from.

Will the legend of Finn MacCool continue? The answer is probably 'yes'. These visitors and their interest may just help the legend of the giant Finn MacCool live for a very long time.

After You Read

1. _____ people come to see the Giant's Causeway every year.
   A. Some
   B. Few
   C. Other
   D. Many

2. Who was Finn MacCool?
   A. a geologist
   B. a giant
   C. a tourist
   D. a tour guide

3. How many pieces of basalt are in the Giant's Causeway?
   A. 40,000
   B. 60 million
   C. 25
   D. 27

4. The word 'used' on page M9 can be replaced by:
   A. dried
   B. made
   C. erupted
   D. moved

5. On page M10, 'he' in paragraph one refers to:
   A. a Scottish giant
   B. Hill Dick
   C. Finn MacCool
   D. a geologist

6. Which is a good heading for page M13?
   A. Wet Mud Makes Columns
   B. Slowly Erupting Lava Turns to Mud
   C. How a Volcano Made the Giant's Causeway
   D. Lava Dries and Shrinks the Mud

7. Geologists think the many-sided columns were made by all of the following ways EXCEPT:
   A. Lava that erupted very quickly.
   B. Wet mud dried on a hot day.
   C. Thick flows of lava.
   D. Lava got smaller while drying.

8. On page M17, the word 'it' refers to:
   A. the causeway
   B. the story
   C. the legend
   D. the science

9. On page M18, the phrase 'tourists and children' can be replaced by:
   A. scientists
   B. tour guides
   C. visitors
   D. geologists

10. The legend of Finn MacCool may last for a very long time because:
    A. The legend is scientific fact.
    B. A lot of children and tourists come to study mythology.
    C. Geologists like to tell the story to tourists.
    D. Visitors like to think about where the causeway came from.

11. The Giant's Causeway is a special place of both _____ and _____.
    A. science, legend
    B. Ireland, Scotland
    C. fact, geologists
    D. story, legend

A Volcano Called VESUVIUS

Herculaneum was a town about five miles south of Naples in Italy. Two thousand years ago, it was a quiet farming center and about five thousand people lived there. It was on the coast and had beautiful views across the sea. In August of the year A.D. 79, everything changed. A nearby volcano called Vesuvius erupted and killed the people in the town. A writer named 'Pliny the Younger' recorded what happened. He was the first person in history ever to describe a volcanic eruption. Because of Pliny's story, Vesuvius is probably the best-known volcano in the world.

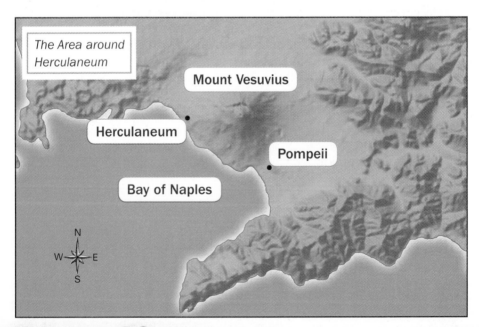

The Area around Herculaneum

Mount Vesuvius

Herculaneum

Pompeii

Bay of Naples

N
W—E
S

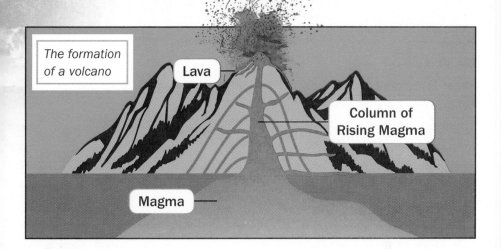

The formation of a volcano

Lava

Column of Rising Magma

Magma

On that August afternoon, most people in the area weren't worried about the volcano. However, suddenly Vesuvius erupted sending hot lava down its sides toward the coast. This lava was fifty feet deep in some places. At the same time, large pieces of rock fell from the volcano. As the hot lava moved quickly toward the town, many people ran to the coast hoping to find safety. However, within four minutes of the first eruption, lava covered the whole town of Herculaneum. Lava also covered the city of Pompeii, a large and important business center nearby.

Scientists now use the term 'Plinean' to describe very fast eruptions like the one that covered Herculaneum. This term comes from the name of Pliny the Younger. Some eruptions are much slower than the one Pliny the Younger described. For example, thousands of tourists visit Hawaii every year to see its quieter volcanoes.

However, it does not matter whether their eruptions are quick or slow, all volcanoes are formed in a similar way. They all begin when magma under the ground starts to move. As it rises, this magma forms a column and then comes out the top of a volcano as lava. Sometimes the lava does not look hot and may move very slowly, but people must always be careful not to get too close.

CD 3, Track 06

Word Count: 312
Time: _____

Vocabulary List

basalt (M: 6)
coast (M: 2, 4, 9, 14)
column (M: 13)
erupt (M: 3, 13)
formation (M: 3, 6, 8, 13, 17)
geologist (M: 3, 10, 13)
giant (M: 2, 3, 4, 6, 9, 10, 12, 13, 14, 17, 18)
Irish (M: 2, 6, 9, 14)
lava (M: 3, 13)
legend (M: 2, 6, 10, 17, 18)
mud (M: 13)
mythology (M: 9)
remind (M: 17)
rock (M: 2, 3, 6, 9, 13, 17)
tour guide (M: 9)
tourist (M: 4, 14, 18)
volcano (M: 3, 9, 10, 14)
weave (M: 17)
World Heritage Site (M: 4)

Snow Magic!

Rob Waring, *Series Editor*

HEINLE
CENGAGE Learning™

Australia • Brazil • Japan • Korea • Mexico • Singapore • Spain • United Kingdom • United States

Words to Know

This story is set the United States (U.S.), in the state of Minnesota. It takes place in a city called Taylors Falls, which is near Minneapolis [mɪniæpəlɪs].

 Weather Words. Here are some weather words you will find in the story. Write the letter of the correct phrase to complete the definitions.

1. Weather is _____.

2. Snow is _____.

3. Winter is _____.

4. Freeze means _____.

5. Temperature is _____.

6. Wind is _____.

a. the season when the weather is coldest

b. white, frozen water that falls from the sky

c. the level of heat or cold

d. the fast, natural movement of air

e. the conditions of the outside environment

f. to become hard at or below 0 degrees Celsius/32 degrees Fahrenheit

Skiing. Read the definitions and look at the picture. Write the number of the correct <u>underlined</u> word next to each item.

1. A <u>ski run</u> is a snow-covered area that people ski on.
2. A <u>mountain</u> is a high area of land.
3. A <u>snow-making machine</u> makes artificial (not real) snow.
4. A <u>skier</u> is a person who moves on snow with long, pieces of wood or plastic, called 'skis.'

A Ski Area

The city of Minneapolis is one of the coldest places in the United States. Winter there usually lasts a very long time. However, even in winter the area sometimes has warmer weather, and that means less snow.

Most people really like this warm weather, but Dan **Raedeke**[1] doesn't like it. He doesn't like it at all! Snow is very important for Raedeke's business. If it's too warm for the snow to stay on the ground, he has a big problem!

---

[1] **Raedeke:** [rədɛki]

 CD 3, Track 07

Predict

Answer the questions. Then read page N7 to check your answers.

1. What is Dan Raedeke's business?

2. What does Raedeke do to get the snow he needs?

Why does Raedeke need snow? He owns the Wild Mountain Ski Area in Taylors Falls, Minnesota. He usually tries to have the ski area completely open by **Thanksgiving**,[2] which is in November. But sometimes, warm weather and a shortage of natural snow cause problems with the ski runs. When this happens, Raedeke can't open until late December!

So, when nature doesn't make snow, Raedeke does. No, it's not **magic**.[3] Raedeke owns the largest snow-making system in the area. He says, "Without snowmaking, we could probably never open ... especially in a year like this. The **fields**[4] are still brown!"

---

[2]**Thanksgiving:** a U.S. national holiday for giving thanks
[3]**magic:** special power that makes impossible things happen
[4]**field:** area of land used for growing food or keeping animals

Snow has always been a very important part of Raedeke's life. His family bought the Wild Mountain Ski Area 28 years ago. Since that time, he's spent nearly every day on the mountain. That experience has helped Raedeke a lot. In addition, Raedeke has also studied **mechanical engineering**.[5] The combination of these two things makes Raedeke kind of a 'specialist' in making snow. He really understands snowmaking and the machines that do it. "Best machine-made snow ever!" he says of his machines. "Look how great that snow is!"

---

[5] **mechanical engineering:** the study of making machines and systems

Snowmaking is kind of a science, but it's also an art, too. It's careful and detailed work. The person making the snow has to carefully measure the water, check the air temperature, and watch the wind. Raedeke explains, "if there's wind, it'll actually **blow**[6] [the water] around and allow it to freeze before it hits the ground. That's why the **snow guns**[7] are always high in the air."

---

[6]**blow:** move with air currents
[7]**snow gun:** a special machine that pushes water into the air to make snow

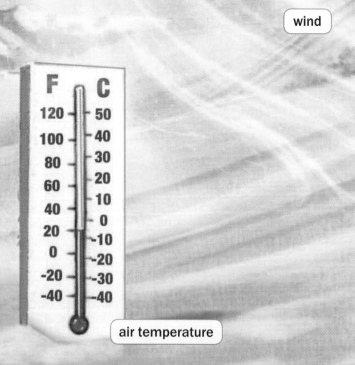

wind

air temperature

snow

water

snow gun

Identify the Main Idea

Skim the previous pages and answer the questions.

1. Why does Raedeke know so much about snowmaking?

2. How does he feel about making snow with machines?

There are good things about both real and man-made snow. However, they are different. Real snow is drier, softer, and of better quality for skiing. But man-made snow lasts for a longer time when there are a lot of people skiing on it.

Raedeke depends on snow for his business. Because of this, he has some of the best snow-making technology available. His newest machines are tall, thin **poles**[8] called 'water sticks.' Raedeke selected them because they produce a lot of snow very quickly. "They make a very soft snow—almost as good as snow from the sky. In one night we can cover this entire **trail**,"[9] he reports. "They're great!" That may be why Raedeke has water sticks on half of the Wild Mountain runs.

---

[8]**pole:** a long wooden or metal rod
[9]**trail:** another word for a ski run; a path

Raedeke then talks about the building that houses the **pumps**[10] for making snow. "This is the **nerve center**[11] of the snow-making system," he says. He explains that it takes good timing to determine which ski runs need snow and which ones don't. He adds that only six pumps control the water that goes through all the **pipes**.[12]

When the water is turned off, Dave Lindgren, the mountain manager, quickly gets the water out of the system. If he doesn't, the pipes might freeze. If a pipe freezes, it's completely useless for the rest of the winter. As he does this, Lindgren also learns a good lesson. Just like all the skiers, he has to be very careful. It's easy to fall down on any kind of snow!

---

[10] **pump:** a machine that forces water to move from one place to another
[11] **nerve center:** a place from which an organization or activity is controlled or managed
[12] **pipe:** a tube through which water or other liquids pass from one place to another

Lindgren goes on to describe the water supply system for Wild Mountain's snow-making operation. Snowmaking needs a lot of water all of the time. So where does all of this water come from?

"This is where we get all our water," says Lindgren. He's talking about the water **reservoir**[13] on top of Wild Mountain. It's a big system. The snow-making process at the ski area needs **3,000 gallons**[14] of water every minute! The reservoir must provide all of this water day after day during warm periods in the winter months.

---

[13] **reservoir:** an man-made lake where water is stored
[14] **3,000 gallons (U.S.):** 11,356 liters

Raedeke is very careful about the snow-making process. He often spends all day and most of the night checking the system. He says, "We check the snow, and we want it like a good snowball." He then picks up a handful of snow. "You can see it's just a little bit wet, and so we'll go to the [snow] gun and turn down the water," he explains. The process requires a lot of care. If there's too much water, the snow gets soft; if there's too little water, the snow doesn't stay on the ground long enough.

To prepare for the next day, Raedeke operates the snow-making machines all night. The ski runs will be covered with new snow in the morning. Wild Mountain will be ready for the day's skiers—with or without nature's help. With good weather, and a little 'snow magic,' Raedeke can keep his skiers happy all winter long!

After You Read

1. In Minneapolis, winter is _____ cold and long.
   A. generally
   B. always
   C. sometimes
   D. never

2. In paragraph 1 on page N7, the word 'completely' can be replaced by:
   A. partly
   B. possibly
   C. totally
   D. nearly

3. Dan Raedeke can't open the ski area when:
   A. The fields are still brown.
   B. The weather is warm.
   C. There is little real snow.
   D. all of the above

4. What is Raedeke's job?
   A. skier
   B. business owner
   C. mechanical engineer
   D. mountain manager

5. In the first sentence on page N10, 'it' refers to:
   A. air temperature
   B. science
   C. wind direction
   D. snowmaking

6. The writer says that snowmaking is an art because:
   A. Water, wind, and air are parts of science.
   B. The snow is artificial.
   C. People must work carefully to make great snow.
   D. The snow guns are high in the air.

7. In paragraph 2 on page N13, the word 'selected' can be replaced by:
    A. decided
    B. chose
    C. liked
    D. needed

8. Raedeke's snow-making machines are good for the following reasons EXCEPT:
    A. They are tall.
    B. They are fast.
    C. They are new.
    D. They are wide.

9. What is the purpose of the last line on page N14?
    A. to explain a surprising event
    B. to show that skiing is dangerous
    C. to worry the reader
    D. to talk about Raedeke's fall

10. When artificial snow doesn't stay on the ground long enough, what is the reason?
    A. It's too wet.
    B. There's too much water.
    C. It's too soft.
    D. There's not enough water.

11. What is NOT part of the snow-making process?
    A. care
    B. water
    C. magic
    D. snow guns

My Visit to the South Pole

December 19

This is going to be a long day. Actually, I'm going to have several very long days. In order to begin my visit to the South Pole, I have a long way to go. First, I have to get from the U.S. to McMurdo Station in Antarctica. I left the house at 5:00 this morning and I won't get to Antarctica for at least three days. It's over nine thousand miles away!

December 22

Well, I'm finally here. We arrived at McMurdo Station at 9:00 last night. It's windy and freezing cold and there is so much snow on the ground. It isn't even winter in Antarctica now! I don't know what the temperature is and I don't want to know. The people with me are a very international group—North Americans, Europeans, and South Americans. Tomorrow we are leaving to go to the South Pole!

The Area around the South Pole

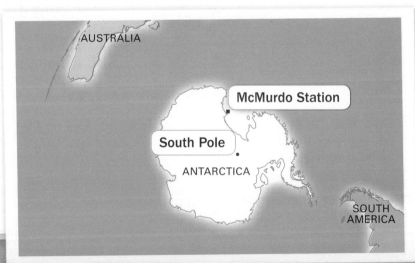

AUSTRALIA

McMurdo Station

South Pole

ANTARCTICA

SOUTH AMERICA

Here I am at the South Pole!

December 24

Here I am at the South Pole! The weather is unbelievably cold.
It's 11:00 at night and it looks like it could be 11:00 in the morning.
There is daylight here for 24 hours a day at this time of year. Can
you believe I just met a group of skiers? They're from Australia
and they're spending nine days skiing around Antarctica, finishing
at the South Pole. I thought my trip was unusual ...

December 27

I'm finally back at McMurdo Station. Thank goodness! Coming back
from the South Pole wasn't as easy as getting there. The weather
was bad and the wind was blowing really hard. It made getting back
to the station very difficult. There were
problems, but I have had a lovely time
here. Right now, however, I'm so cold!
My warm bed is going to be a great
ending to a wonderful few days ...

 CD 3, Track 08

Word Count: 315
Time: _____

Vocabulary List

blow (N: 10)
field (N: 7)
freeze (N: 2, 10, 14)
magic (N: 7, 18)
mechanical engineering (N: 8)
mountain (N: 3, 7, 8, 13, 14, 17, 18)
nerve center (N: 14)
pipe (N: 14, 15)
pole (N: 13)
pump (N: 14, 15)
reservoir (N: 17)
ski run (N: 3, 7, 14, 18)
skier (N: 3, 14, 18)
snow (N: 2, 3, 4, 5, 7, 8, 10, 11, 12, 13, 14, 17, 18)
snow gun (N: 10, 11)
snow-making machine (N: 3, 18)
temperature (N: 2, 10)
trail (N: 13)
weather (N: 2, 4, 7, 18)
wind (N: 2, 10)
winter (N: 2, 4, 14, 17, 18)

Volcano
TREK

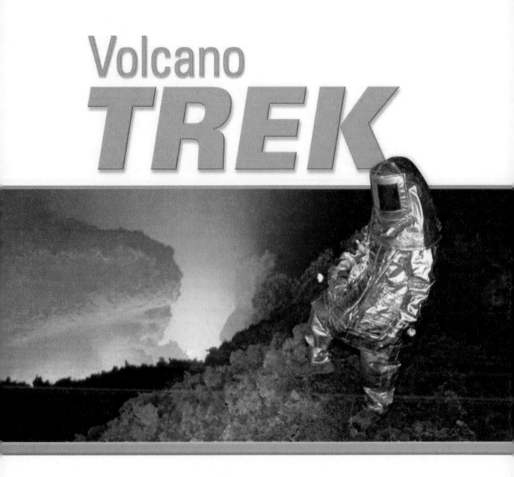

Rob Waring, *Series Editor*

HEINLE
CENGAGE Learning™

Australia • Brazil • Japan • Korea • Mexico • Singapore • Spain • United Kingdom • United States

Words to Know

This story is set in Africa, in the country of Ethiopia. It happens in the Afar [afar] region near a volcano called Erta Ale [ɜrtə ɑlə].

A **A Volcano.** Read the paragraph. Then, label the picture with the <u>underlined</u> words.

A volcano is a mountain with a large hole at the top. This hole is called a <u>crater</u>. In an <u>eruption</u>, a volcano produces very hot, melted rock. When it is under the ground, this hot, melted rock is called <u>magma</u>. Once it comes out of the volcano, the hot rock is called <u>lava</u>. Sometimes lava comes together in the crater. This is called a <u>lava lake</u>.

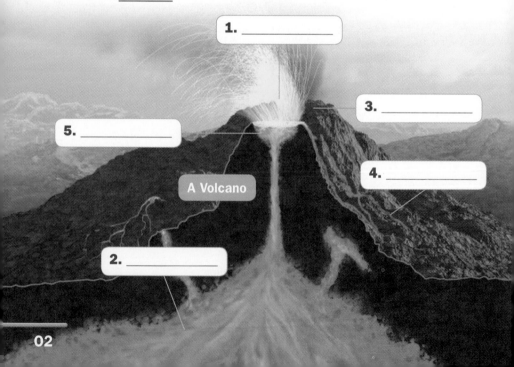

1. _____

3. _____

5. _____

4. _____

A Volcano

2. _____

B Volcano Explorers. Read the paragraph. Then, match each word with the correct definition.

   This story is about two explorers from Nice [nis], France, Franck Tessier [fɾɑŋk tɛsyeɪ] and Irene Margaritis [aɪɾin mɑɾɡəɾitɪs]. These explorers are geologists who are trekking to the Erta Ale volcano. They ride camels to get to the volcano because it is difficult to reach it. Volcanoes can be dangerous. The geologists want to study the volcano's lava, rocks, and soil. They want to learn more about volcanoes and how they work. This information may help people and save lives.

1. explorers _____

2. geologists _____

3. trek _____

4. camels _____

5. dangerous _____

a. make a long, difficult journey

b. scientists who study Earth

c. not safe

d. large animals that often carry people or things

e. people who travel to new places to learn new things

The Earth

Rocks and Soil

Millions of years ago, **man's earliest ancestors**[1] lived in Africa, in a far region of Ethiopia. Here in this area is the Erta Ale volcano. Hot lava has erupted from this volcano for about one hundred years. The temperature of the lava here is more than **2,000 degrees Fahrenheit**.[2]

Now, a team of explorers is going to explore Erta Ale for themselves. They want to learn more about the volcano. However, it's not an easy trek, and the team has to use camels to get to the area. The camels are able to carry the team and the heavy things they need for their research.

---

[1]**man's earliest ancestors:** some of the first people on Earth
[2]**2,000 degrees Fahrenheit:** 1093° (degrees) Celsius

 CD 3, Track 09

The explorers and their camels finally reach the crater of the Erta Ale volcano. Franck Tessier and Irene Margaritis are **professors**[3] at the University of Nice in France. They're geologists, or scientists who study the earth. They have traveled halfway around the world just to see the Erta Ale volcano. They are hoping that they'll find something very interesting. They want to find data that will tell them about the history of Earth.

---

[3] **professor:** teacher at a university or college

The geologists look down into the volcano. Deep in the crater, they can see the black lava lake of Erta Ale. Professor Margaritis is very happy to finally be here. "It is quite **exciting**.[4] I want to see it now," she says. Very soon, they will go into the crater and look at the lava more closely. But why is the Erta Ale volcano so special for geologists?

---

[4]**exciting:** causing a very happy feeling

Infer Meaning

1. Why is Professor Margaritis happy?
2. What does she mean by 'it' in "I want to see it now"?

The Erta Ale volcano is in the Afar area of Ethiopia. The Afar **triangle**[5] is in an area where three **continental plates**[6] meet. These plates move farther and farther apart every year. Because of this, it's an area that's always changing.

Erta Ale has the oldest lava lake in the world. The lake is also one of the lowest points on Earth. At Erta Ale, geologists can study how the world began millions of years ago. That's why this place is so special.

---

[5]**triangle:** an area with three sides
[6]**continental plates:** geologist's term for the large pieces of rock far under the ground

Continental Plates

Afar Triangle

011

A lava lake is a mixture of hot and cooler lava. Very hot lava comes out of the earth. This lava forms the base of Erta Ale's lava lake. As this lava **cools down**,[7] it becomes hard and black. However, a lava lake is a place of change and movement. Soon, hot magma breaks through this covering as the volcano erupts again and again. Erta Ale is an active volcano and it's fair to say that it could have a big eruption at almost any time!

---

[7] **cools down:** becomes cold

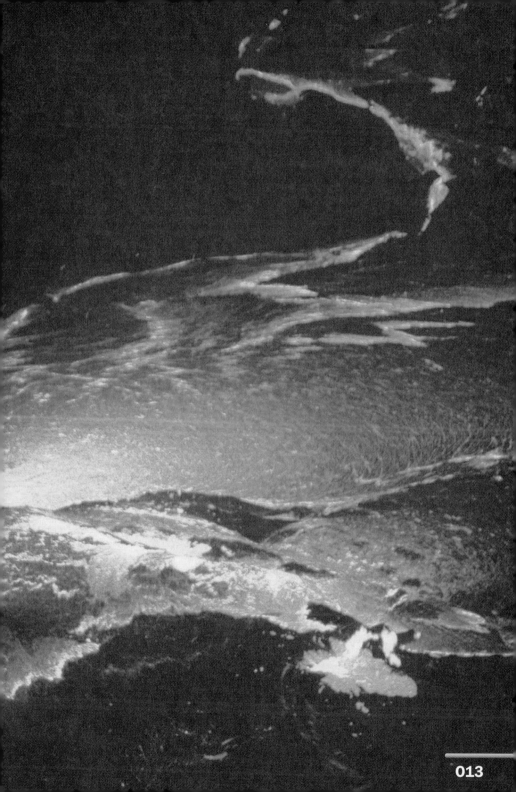
013

The geologists stand at the top of this active volcano and wait at the side of the crater. It's very interesting for them, but it's not easy to be here. There's a very strong smell of **sulfur**[8] in the air. And even in the early morning, it's already very, very hot.

It soon gets even hotter as the group goes slowly and carefully down into the crater. Professor Tessier wants to collect **samples**[9] of the red-hot lava near the lava lake. The team spends many hours down by the lake.

---

[8]**sulfur:** a yellow material that smells very bad
[9]**sample:** a small amount

It's a very long day for the geologists. In fact, it's two o'clock in the morning when they return from the crater. They have all worked very hard. Professor Margaritis has only one thing to say about the trek; "very hot," she says with a smile.

Everyone is pleased with the lava samples the team brings back from the crater. "I think this is **fresh**[10] lava," Tessier says about his samples. He then explains to the team that the pieces didn't come directly from the lava lake. However, the team decides the samples are fresh enough and they put them in a bag. The geologists will analyze these samples later.

_____

[10] **fresh:** new

After a difficult trek, the team finally has their samples of lava. They will now leave Erta Ale and go back to study the lava. What do they want to learn? As professors, Margaritis and Tessier want to learn new information that they can teach to others. However, as geologists, they also want to know what the lava of Erta Ale may teach them. The lava may help them to understand more about Erta Ale, about volcanoes in general, and about how the world began millions of years ago.

Summarize

Summarize the story of the volcano trek.
Tell it to a partner or write it in a notebook.
Include the following information:

- Who went on the trek?

- What did they want to see?

- Where did they go?

- Why did they want to go there?

After You Read

1. Hot lava has erupted from Erta Ale for how many years?
   A. millions of years
   B. about 100 years
   C. more than 2,000 years
   D. 1,000,000 years

2. Why does the team use camels to get to the volcano?
   A. Camels like volcanoes.
   B. Camels can reach 2,000 degrees Fahrenheit.
   C. Camels are fast animals.
   D. Camels can carry many things.

3. On page O7, what data does the team want to collect?
   A. data about the history of the earth
   B. data about the temperature of the volcano
   C. data about how long the volcano has been erupting
   D. data on all of the above

4. Professor Margaritis is _____ excited about being at the lava lake.
   A. a little
   B. very
   C. not
   D. never

5. What is the writer's purpose on page O10?
   A. to show that Erta Ale is in a triangle
   B. to teach about Ethiopia's towns
   C. to tell more about the Erta Ale volcano
   D. to teach why the continental plates are moving together

6. What is a good heading for page O12?
   A. Lava Lakes Made from Cool Lava
   B. Erta Ale Is a Safe Volcano.
   C. How a Lava Lake Forms.
   D. A Long, Hot Trek to the Crater

7. Which does NOT happen at the Erta Ale volcano?
   A. Cool magma makes a lava lake.
   B. Lava comes out from deep in the earth.
   C. Lava cools down.
   D. Hot magma erupts again and again.

8. What does 'collect' mean on page O14?
   A. see
   B. bring
   C. get
   D. touch

9. Which is NOT a good heading for page O16?
   A. 2:00 a.m. Return from Volcano
   B. Geologists Go Down into Crater
   C. Tired Professors Worked Hard
   D. Hot Trek Makes Explorers Tired

10. When the team decides the samples are 'fresh enough,' they mean that they're:
   A. old
   B. not acceptable
   C. cold
   D. OK to use

11. The explorers are excited to _____ from and _____ about the lava.
   A. know, study
   B. taught, studied
   C. learn, teach
   D. teach, teach

MAN VS. VOLCANO:
Can there be a winner?

S cientists tell us that the earth currently has about seventy active volcanoes. Right now, there are probably about twenty volcanic eruptions happening in the world. Some of these eruptions are large and some are very small, but all of them can be deadly.

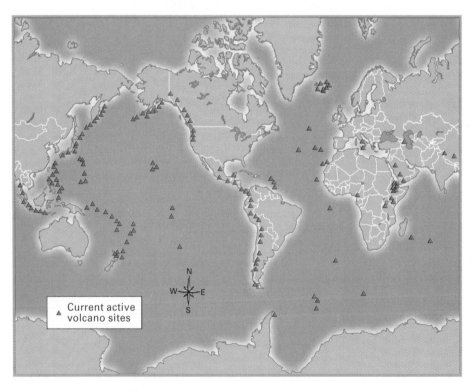

A Map of Current Active Volcano Sites

Current active volcano sites

The number of people on Earth is increasing. As a result, people often find themselves living in dangerous areas near volcanoes. Over three million people live near Mount Rainer in the U.S. Another one million people live near Mount Etna in Sicily, Italy. It is quite possible that either of these areas may experience a volcanic eruption in the future.

For centuries, scientists have tried different ways of protecting people from volcanoes. They have tried:

- Stopping the eruption (This was impossible.)

- Forcing the lava to move away from where people live (This was difficult to do.)

- Asking people not to live near volcanoes (This has not worked.)

- Making plans for people to leave the area of an eruption quickly (This sometimes works.)

None of these ideas were particularly effective.

Geologists are now trying to find new ways to know when a volcano is going to erupt. They know that most volcanic activity happens near the sides of continental plates. These plates are always coming together or moving away from one another. When a lot of magma pushes up under moving plates, we often see a volcanic eruption. Geologists also know that before the eruption happens, something called 'lahar' starts moving under the ground. Lahar is made from hot water, magma and pieces of stone. Geologists are now using a machine that is placed under the ground. This machine keeps a record of the movement of the lahar. When there are a lot of quick movements, scientists know that an eruption is likely to happen.

CD 3, Track 10

Word Count: 302
Time: _____

Vocabulary List

camel (O: 3, 4, 7)

continental plate (O: 10)

cool down (O: 12)

crater (O: 2, 7, 8, 14, 16)

dangerous (O: 3)

eruption (O: 2, 12)

exciting (O: 8)

explorer (O: 3, 4, 7)

fresh (O: 16)

geologist (O: 3, 7, 8, 10, 14, 16, 19)

lava (O: 2, 4, 8, 12, 14, 16, 19)

lava lake (O: 2, 8, 10, 12, 14)

magma (O: 2, 12)

man's earliest ancestors (O: 4)

professor (O: 7, 8, 9, 14, 16, 19)

sample (O: 14, 16, 19)

sulfur (O: 14)

trek (O: 3, 4, 19)

triangle (O: 10)

Credits

Arctic Whale Danger!

Photography Credits:
TP ©Art Wolfe/Getty Images, A4 ©AFP/Getty Images, A4-5 ©A.G.E. Foto Stock/First Light, A8-9 ©Image Source 2005/Getty Images, A10-11 ©Norbert Rosing/National Geographic, A12-13 ©David Fleetham/Alamy, A14-15 ©Flip Nicklin/Getty Images, A15 © Bryan & Cherry Alexander Photography/Alamy, A18-19 © Flip Nicklin/Getty Images, A22-23 ©Ira Block/National Geographic

Illustration Credits:
A2 (t) © Mapping Specialists, A2 (br) © Tom Connell, A3 (br) © Tom Connell, A6-7 © Tom Connell, A16-17 © Tom Connell.

Happy Elephants

Photography Credits:
TP © Beverly Joubert/National Geographic Image Collection, B4 © Ann-Marie Palmer/Alamy, B4-5 © Joel Sartore/Getty Images, B8-9 © Michael Fay/National Geographic Image Collection, B10-11 © Roy Toft/Getty Images, B12-13 © Kelly-Mooney Photography/Corbis, B13 © George D. Lepp/Photo Researchers, Inc., B16-17 © Nigel J. Dennis/Photo Researchers, Inc., B17 © Beverly Joubert/National Geographic Image Collection, B18 © Clumsy Ball/Alamy, B18-19 © BIOS Denis-Huot M. & C. /Peter Arnold, Inc., B22 © Nature and Wildlife/PhotoDisc, B23 © blickwinkel /Alamy.

Illustration Credits:
B2 (t) © Mapping Specialists, ltd. Madison, WI, USA, B2-3 © 80b Kayganich/IllustrationOnLine.com, B6-7 © Bob Kayganich/IllustrationOnLine.com, B14-15 © Bob Kayganich/IllustrationOnLine.com.

Monkey Party

Photography Credits:
TP © Dan Vincent/Alamy, C4 © Paula Bronstein/Getty Images, C5 © Cyril Ruoso/BIOS/Peter Arnold, C6-7 © Paula Bronstein/Getty Images, C8-9 © Paula Bronstein/Getty Images, C12 © Dan White/Alamy, C13 © Adam Deschamps/Alamy, C14-15 © SAEED KHAN/Getty Images, C16-17 © AFP/Getty Images, C22 (t) © PhotoDisc/CD-Backgrounds and Textures, C22 (b) © Angelo Hornak/CORBIS, C23 © Sami Sarkis/Getty Images.

Illustration Credits:
C2 (t) © Mapping Specialists, Ltd. Madison, WI, USA, C2-3 © Patrick Gnan/IllustrationOnLine.com, C10-11 © Sharon and Joel Harris/illustrationOnLine.com, C18-19 © Sharon and Joel Harris/illustrationOnLine.com.

The Future of a Village

Photography Credits:
TP © Oliver DIGOIT/Alamy, D6-7 © Michael Setboun/Corbis, D8-9 © Dougie Wallace/Alamy, D12-13 © Yadid Levy/Alamy, D14 © Heather Perry/National Geographic Image Collection, D14-1S © Nick Hanna/Alamy, D16-17 © Ian Cumming/Getty Images, D18-19 © Simon Bottomley/Getty Images, D22 (t) © David Olsen/Getty Images, D22 (b) © Cartesia/Getty Images, D23 © G Brad Lewis/Getty Images.

Illustration Credits:
D2 (t) © Mapping Specialists, Ltd. Madison, WI, USA, D2-3, D4-5,D10-11 © Mark Gerber.

Credits (continued)

Life on the Orinoco

Photography Credits:
TP © Woody Stock/Alamy, E4 © MARK EDWARDS/Peter Arnold, Inc., E4-5 © Aurora/Getty Images, E6-7 © Tom Till/Getty Images, E10-11 © Morales/First Light, E12 © Shafer & Hill/Peter Arnold, Inc., E12-13 © Shafer & Hill/Getty Images, E14-15 © Aurora/Getty Images, E18 © Image State/Alamy, E18-19 © Robert Caputo/Getty Images, E22 (t) © PhotoDisc/CDBusiness and Industry.

Illustration Credits:
E2 (t) © Mapping Specialists, Ltd. Madison, WI, USA, E2-3, E8-9, E16-17 © Alan Male for American Artists Rep., Inc., E22 (b) © Mapping Specialists, Ltd. Madison, WI, USA.

The Lost City of Machu Picchu

Photography Credits:
TP © Ed Simpson/Getty Images, F4-5 © Darrell Gulin/Corbis, F5 © George D. Lepp/Corbis, F6-7 © PILAR OLIVARES/Reuters/Corbis, F10 © Bettmann/CORBIS, F10-11 © Bob Krist/CORBIS, F12-13 © Reuters/Corbis, F14-15 © Crispin Rodwell/Alamy, F18-19 © John Van Hasselt/CORBIS SYGMA, F22 © George D. Lepp/CORBIS, F23 © John Van Hasselt/CORBIS SYGMA.

Illustration Credits:
F2 (t) © Mapping Specialists, Ltd. Madison, WI, USA, F2-3 © Jim Effler for American Artists Rep., Inc., F8-9 © Jim Effler for American Artists Rep., Inc., F16-17 © Jim Effler for American Artists Rep., Inc.

Columbus and the New World

Photography Credits:
TP © Kean Collection/Getty Images, G6-7 © Jon Arnold Images/Alamy, G7 © North Wind Picture Archives/Alamy, G8 © Bettmann/CORBIS, G8-9 © Bettmann/CORBIS, G10-11 © North Wind/North Wind Picture Archives, G12-13 © Bettmann/CORBIS, G16-17 © North Wind/North Wind Picture Archives, G17 © North Wind Picture Archives/Alamy, G18-19 © Archivo Iconografico, SA/Corbis, G22 © Mapping Specialists, Ltd. Madison, WI, USA, G23 © Chad Ehlers/Alamy.

Illustration Credits:
G2 (t) © Mapping Specialists, Ltd. Madison, WI, USA, G2-3, G4-5, G14-15 © Mike Jarosko for American Artists Rep., Inc., G20 © Mapping Specialists, Ltd. Madison, WI, USA.

Dreamtime Painters

Photography Credits:
TP © Chris McLennan/Alamy, H4 ©Nat Photos/Getty Images, H4-5 © Thorsten Milse/Getty Images, H6-7 © Michael and Patricia Fogden/CORBIS, H10-11 © Charles and Josette Lenars/CORBIS, H14-15 © Charles and Josette Lenars/CORBIS, H16-17 © Penny Tweedie/Getty Images, H18-19 © LOOK Die Bildagentur der Fotografen GmbH/Alamy, H22 (t) © PhotoDisc/CD-Backgrounds and Textures, H22 (b) © Mapping Specialists, Ltd. Madison, WI, USA, H23 © Sisse Brimberg/Getty Images.

Illustration Credits:
H2 (t) © Mapping Specialists, Ltd. Madison, WI, USA, H2-3, H8-9, H12-13 © Space Channel for American Artists Rep., Inc.

The Young Riders of Mongolia

Photography Credits:

TP © James L Stanfield/National Geographic Image Collection, I4-5 © Barry Lewis/Corbis, I6 © Dennis Cox/Alamy, Michael Reynolds/epa/Corbis, I10 © Christoph & Friends/Das Fotoarchiv/Alamy, I10-11 © KEERLE GEORGES DE/CORBIS SYGMA, I12-13 © Gordon Wiltsie/Getty Images, I14-15 © James L Stanfield/National Geographic Image Collection, I18-19 © David Edwards/National Geographic Image Collection.

Illustration Credits:

I2 (t) Mapping Specialists, Ltd. Madison, WI, USA, I2-3 © Mark Gerber, I8-9 © Mark Gerber, I16-17 © Mark Gerber.

Alaskan Ice Climbing

Photography Credits:

TP © Joel Sartore/National Geographic Image Collection, J4-5 © Danita Delimont /Alamy, J6-7 © Medford Taylor/National Geographic Image Collection, J8 © MIMOTITO/Getty Images, J9 © WorldFoto/Alamy, J10-11 © Panoramic Images/National Geographic Image Collection, J11 © Chad Case/Alamy, J14-15 © Alaska Stock LLC/Alamy, J18-19 © Paul A. Souders/CORBIS, J22 © James Balog/Getty Images, J22-23 © PhotoDisc/CD-Elements, J23 © blickwinkel/Alamy.

Illustration Credits:

J2 (t) © Mapping Specialists, Ltd. Madison, WI, USA, J2-3 © Jim Effler for American Artists Rep., Inc., J12-13 © Jim Effler for American Artists Rep., Inc., J16-17 © Jim Effler for American Artists Rep., Inc.

Don't Believe Your Eyes!

Photography Credits:

TP © Ronald R. Johnson/Getty Images, K2 (bl) © JODI COBB/National Geographic Image Collection, K4-5 © Ronald R. Johnson/Getty Images, K8-9 © Ruth Tomlinson/Getty Images, K10-11 © Arne Hodalic/Corbis, K14-15 © John Ferro Sims/Alamy, K16-17 © John Ferro Sims/Alamy, K18-19 © John and Lisa Merrill/Corbis, K22 (t) © photoDisc/CO-Nature and Environment, K22 (b) © Michael Busselle/Getty Images, K23 © Chad Ehlers/Alamy.

Illustration Credits:

K2 (t) © Mapping Specialists, Ltd. Madison, WI, USA, K2 (br), K3, K6-7, K12, K13 © Space Channel for American Artists Rep., Inc.

The Story of the Hula

Photography Credits:

TP © Steve Raymer/National Geographic Image Collection, L4-5 © Steve Raymer/National Geographic Image Collection, L8 © Paul Chesley/Getty Images, L9 © Zee/Alamy, L10 © Photo Resource Hawaii/Alamy, L10-11 © LYNN JOHNSON/National Geographic Image Collection, L12 © Scott Kemper/Alamy, L13 © Photo Resource Hawaii/Alamy, L14-15 © Steve Raymer/National Geographic Image Collection, L18-19 © Paul Spinelli/Getty Images, L22 © Blaine Harrington Ili/Alamy.

Illustration Credits:

L2 (t) © Mapping Specialists, Ltd. Madison, WI, USA, L2-3, L6-7,L16-17 © Jim Effler - American Artists Rep., Inc.

Credits (continued)

The Giant's Causeway

Photography Credits:

TP © Charles Bowman/Robert Harding World Imagery/Corbis, M4-5 © Glen Allison/Getty Images, M6 © IT Stock Free/SuperStock, M7 © Alan Becker/Getty Images, M10-11 © Westend 61/Alamy, M14 © Steve Vidler/SuperStock, M14-15 © Atlanpic/Alamy, M16 © Richard Murphy/Alamy, M17 © Marshal Ikonography/Alamy, M18-19 © Andrew Holt/Alamy, M22 (t) © PhotoDisc/CD-Nature, Wildlife and Environment.

Illustration Credits:

M2 (t) © Mapping Specialists, Ltd. Madison, WI, USA, M2 © Mark Snyder for American Artists Rep., Inc., M3 © Mark Snyder for American Artists Rep., Inc., M8-9 © Mark Snyder for American Artists Rep., Inc., M12-13 © Mark Snyder for American Artists Inc., M22 (b) © Mapping Specialists, Ltd. Madison, WI, USA.

Snow Magic!

Photography Credits:

TP © Mike Goldwater/Alamy, N4 © wsr/Alamy, N4-5 © Richard Hamilton Smith/CORBIS, N6-7 © Layne Kennedy/CORBIS, N8 © Sebastien Baussais/Alamy, N8-9 © Layne Kennedy/CORBIS, N12-13 © Chris Selby/Alamy, N16-17 © Layne Kennedy/CORBIS, N18-19 © Marina Jefferson/Getty Images, N22 (t) © PhotoDisc/CD-Nature, Wildlife and Environment, N23 © Jeff Harbers/Getty Images.

Illustration Credits:

N2 (t) © Mapping Specialists, Ltd. Madison, WI, USA, N2-3, N10-11, N14-15 © Jim Effler for American Artists Rep., Inc., N22 (b) © Mapping Specialists, Ltd. Madison, WI, USA,.

Volcano Trek

Photography Credits:

TP © CARSTEN PETER/National Geographic Image Collection, O4-5 © Bobby Haas/Getty Images, O6-7 © Carsten Peter/Getty Images, O7 © Maria Stenzel/Getty Images, O8-9 © blickwinkel/Alamy, O12 © Tony Waltham/Robert Harding World Imagery/Corbis, O12-13 © Carsten Peter/Getty Images, O16-17 © CARSTEN PETER/National Geographic Image Collection, O18-19 © CARSTEN PETER/National Geographic Image Collection, O22-23 (t) © PhotoDisc/CD-Science and Technology, O22 (b) © Mapping Specialists, Ltd. Madison, WI, USA.

Illustration Credits:

O2 (t) © Mapping Specialists, Ltd. Madison, WI, USA, O2-3, O10-11, O14-15 © Bob Kayganich/ IliustrationOnLine.com.